This Page is Blank

Materials were not available when scanned.

A

STATISTICAL AND DESCRIPTIVE ACCOUNT

OF

THE SEVERAL COUNTIES

OF THE

State of North Carolina,

UNITED STATES OF AMERICA.

PUBLISHED BY THE NORTH CAROLINA LAND COMPANY.

RALEIGH:

NICHOLS & GORMAN, BOOK AND JOB PRINTERS.

1869.

NORTH CAROLINA

LAND COMPANY,

ESTABLISHED FOR THE

TRANSPORTATION AND LOCATION

OF

Northern and European Settlers

IN THE

STATE OF NORTH CAROLINA,

FOR THE

SALE OF REAL ESTATE,

Agricultural Implements, Machinery, &c., &c.

—ALSO—

Negotiate Loans on Mortgages and other Securities.

Chartered by Act of General Assembly, 1869.

OFFICERS:

Geo. Little, President. **R. W. Best, Secretary.**

DIRECTORS:

AT RALEIGH.

Hon. R. W. Best, late Sec. of State.
Col. Geo. Little, late U. S. Marshal.
Geo. W. Swepson, Ral. Nat. Bank.
R. Kingsland, late of N. Y. City.

AT NEW YORK.

A. J. Bleecker, Esq.

AGENTS AT NEW YORK AND BOSTON.

A. J. Bleecker, Son & Co.,
77, Cedar Street,
New York City.

TO THE READER.

This publication has been gotten up at considerable expense and labor, at the instance and under the supervision of the North Carolina Land Company, which is composed of a number of intelligent, enterprising and respectable gentlemen of the States of New York and North Carolina.

This Company has been established in this city for the purpose of aiding in the transportation and location of Northern and European settlers coming to North Carolina, and for the sale of lands of all descriptions, suited to the wants of the agriculturist, the vine and fruit grower, the truck farmer, the miner and manufacturer, as well as the sale of improved and unimproved lots in the towns and cities of the State, and to render all possible assistance to persons who desire to invest their funds in this State, judiciously.

In order to furnish to persons desirous of coming to the State, the most reliable, general and statistical information, as a guide to investment and location, the Land Company has procured the services of gentlemen in no way interested personally in their enterprise, who, from long acquaintance and actual observation, were well qualified to give a brief but correct description of every county. Besides this, they have procured a mass of valuable information in the form of letters, from leading gentlemen who have held high public positions in the State, and whose thorough acquaintance with the subjects upon which they write, as well as their entire reliability, remove all doubt as to the truthfulness and correctness of their statements. The whole, therefore, embodies an amount of information precisely suited to the wishes of all classes of persons who desire to seek a home, in one of the most highly favored portions of the earth, in climate, soil, natural advantages, capacity for improvement, population, &c., which cannot be obtained from any other publication.

Intelligent gentlemen who have made themselves acquainted by personal observation, with the population, climate, soil, productions and capacity for improvement of every portion of the United States, do not hesitate to declare, since the close of the rebellion, that the Southern States offer vastly superior inducements both for investment and location, to those of he Northwestern States and Territories, whither the tide of emigration has been so strongly tending in late years. Unprejudiced travellers who have visited North Carolina, after a short stay in the State, invariably express a preference for the Old North State, to that of any other. Thousands of her children, who in the spirit of money-making left the State years ago to try their fortunes in the West, South or North, are returning to their native soil, and thousands more are meditating a return when their circumstances will allow it.

The world does not possess any where a more quiet, peaceable, honest and frugal population, than the people of this State. Notwithstanding the devastation, ruin and demoralization of the late civil war, our people are rapidly returning to their old customs and labors. A more law-abiding people cannot be found. Foreigners and strangers who come among us to engage in the industrial and business professions of life and to pursue the arts of peace, are everywhere hailed with joy, and the aim and desire of our people generally, is to promote peace and quietude, enterprise and prosperity among all classes, and to encourage and support wise laws and a good government, which give the greatest security and protection to life, labor and property.

The State covers an area of 34,000,000 of acres, stretching nearly 500 miles from the Atlantic Ocean to the Tennessee line, and from 150 to 100 miles from the Virginia to the South Carolina and Georgia lines. Within this area there is almost every variety of soil and climate. Physically, the State is divided into three departments, differing in soil, climate and production. The Eastern division stretches along the Atlantic coast and nearly extends westwardly to a line drawn North and South through the Capital of the State. This section abounds in navigable sounds, rivers and creeks, in which fish are abundant. The shad and herring fisheries are sources of great profit. The soil is either rich loam, or sandy land, or extensive swamp rich lands. The sandy lands abound in pine forests, from which turpentine and tar are made; are easily cultivated and improved; are not naturally very productive; but when improved give a profitable return in cotton, corn, potatoes (sweet), peas, pea-nuts, grapes and vegetables of all kinds. The rich lands, whether up-land or swamp, are very productive. Some of these lands produce a bale of picked cotton to the acre, or 75 to 100 bushels of Indian corn. This whole eastern section, is flat and damp, but will produce cotton and corn in great abundance, and is finely adapted to truck farming. The pine and cypress timber of this whole section is immensely valuable. The North-eastern counties are valuable for fisheries, fine cypress timber, and are equal to any for Indian corn, wheat, vineyards, &c. The middle and southern counties of this region, embrace the best cotton portions of the State, and are valuable for fisheries, timber, corn, truck farming, pea-nuts, vineyards, &c., being contiguous to market by Rail Road and water communication. Like all low countries, it is subject to malarious diseases, such as bilious fever and ague and fever. Good drainage and proper care, however, make it a healthy and desirable region. It is perhaps superior to any section of the United States, in affording a good living for the smallest amount of labor. This region will become famous as a grape growing and wine making country.

The middle or second department is undulating and hilly, growing more so as you approach the mountains. The eastern and southern counties of this department, abound in lands from ordinary to good, and are productive of cotton, corn, wheat, potatoes, fruits of all kinds, &c. They are generally very healthy, with good pure water, and intersected with Rail Roads. Mines of coal, iron, gold and copper are numerous, and water-power is abundant for manufacturing. The northern and western counties of this department produce tobacco, corn, wheat and the grasses, finely.

The Western department embraces the mountain region, which is capable of being made one of the finest grazing countries in the world. Horses, cattle, sheep and swine are raised in large numbers. As a wool growing region, it is very superior. Here, also, mines of gold, copper and iron abound and the water power is unsurpassed. It is a bleak but exceedingly healthy region, and Indian corn, wheat, rye, barley and fruits grow well. But for further and more specific information, we refer the reader to the description given of each County in the body of the work, and to the letters before alluded to.

Besides the general character of our population, the salubrity of our climate, the variety, productiveness and improvability of our soil, our mining and manufacturing advantages and our Rail Roads, all well calculated to interest and invite the traveller, we can point to the educational advantages of the State with great pride. Besides the University of the State, there are five or six Male Colleges of high grade, together with a number of first class high schools and academies in full operation. In female education this State is not behind any in the liberality of its provisions. There are about twenty Female Colleges and High Schools in the State. Formerly the State provided quite liberally for Common or Public School instruction for all the white children of the State. Under the new order of things, a still more liberal provision will be made for all the children of the State, without regard to color or condition. White and black will be, however, educated in separate schools.

With this brief outline of the general characteristics of the State, we shall not longer detain the reader from the body of the work.

THE EDITOR.

Raleigh, N. C., April 15, 1869.

STATISTICAL

AND

DESCRIPTIVE ACCOUNT OF COUNTIES, &C.

ALAMANCE.

This county was taken from the western part of Orange county, in 1848. It lies in the middle tier of counties and is bounded N. by Caswell county, E. by Orange, S. by Chatham and W. by Guilford.

Area, 500 square miles.

Population 11,000.

Farms, 923; acres improved, 98,250; acres unimproved, 115,000.

Natural growth of trees: maple, white, red and chestnut oak, hickory and walnut.

Annual products: corn, about 500,000 bushels; wheat, 82,000 bushels; oats, 11,000 bushels; hay, 3,785 tons; cotton, 150 bales; tobacco, 15,000 pounds; butter, 100,000 pounds; fruits and vegetables, abundant.

Stock: horses and mules, 3,335; cattle, 8,000; sheep, 8,500; hogs, 22,500.

Schools: Col. Bingham's, at Mebanesville; Rev. Mr. Long's, and Rev. A. Currie's, at Graham; male and female academy at Company Shops, and others.

Churches, 33.

Lawyers, 3; doctors, 12; mills, 15; cotton factories, 5; post offices, 14.

This county is watered by Saxapahaw river and Alamance, Mary's Bark and other creeks. The surface is undulating; soil, highly productive; farms good, and low grounds rich.

The North Carolina Central Rail Road connecting the Eastern and Western portions of the State, runs through this county.

Company Shops, where the North Carolina Rail Road has its offices and engine and car works, is a pretty place, and gives promise of great future prosperity.

GRAHAM, the county seat, named after Gov. Graham, is about 58 miles west of Raleigh.

ALEXANDER.

This county was formed from Iredell, Wilkes and Caldwell counties in 1846. It is in the mountain region.

Area, 300 square miles.

Population, 6,250. It is drained by the Yadkin, Mitchell and Little Rivers and several creeks.

Farms, 653; acres improved, 30,000; acres unimproved, 105,000.

Annual products: corn, 165,000 bushels; wheat, 10,000 bushels; rye and oats, 40,000 bushels; Irish and sweet potatoes, 30,000 bushels; peas and beans, 3,000 bushels; butter, 32,000 pounds; flax, 12,000 pounds; cotton, 15,000 pounds; wool, 15,000 pounds; honey and beeswax, 12,000 pounds.

Native forests: oak, walnut, beach, maple, poplar and chestnut.

Stock: horses and mules, 1,380; cattle, 3,599; sheep, 5,112; hogs, 10,056.

Churches, 20. Schools: Cheoway Academy; York Institute; Elk Shoal Academy; United Baptist Institute and many others. Cotton factory, 1; mills, 14. Tanneries, several.

This county is surrounded by mountains, and abounds in mineral springs, chiefly chalybeate and sulphur. Climate, healthy. Land productive.

TAYLORSVILLE, the county seat, is 150 miles west from Raleigh.

ALLEGHANY.

This county, lately formed from the eastern part of Ashe, lies between the Blue Ridge and the Virginia line.

Area, about 290 square miles.

Churches, 16; ministers, 13; Lawyer, 1; College, Alleghany, at Gap Civil; Schools, at various points; post offices, 4; mills, 6; mines, in numerous places.

Farms, 390.

Annual products: corn, 100,000 bushels; wheat, 3,000 bushels; rye and oats, 75,000 bushels; buckwheat, 3,000 bushels; pease, 12,000 bushels; Irish and sweet potatoes, 1,500 bushels; butter and cheese, 6,500 pounds; flax seed, 500 bushels; flax, 12,500 pounds; maple sugar, 5,000 pounds; tobacco, 2,500 pounds; wool, 14,000 pounds; honey and beeswax, 12,000 pounds; hay, 4,000 tons; fruits, in value, $500.

Trees, natural growth: white, Spanish and chestnut oaks, and black and white pine.

Mountains: Fisher's Gap, Elk Spur, Lame Spring, Peach Bottom and Saddle.

Rivers; New and Little.

Creeks: Crab, Glade, Prather's, Elk, Chestnut, Brush, Big Pine and others.

Climate, cool and healthy. Soil, good. Fine grazing country.

SPARTA, the county seat, is about 200 miles from Raleigh.

ANSON.

This county, named from Admiral Anson of the British Navy, was formed in 1740, and extended at that time to the western limits of the State.

Area, 650 square miles.

Population, 13,000.

Farms, 675; acres improved, 93,965; acres unimproved, 213,-167.

Annual products; corn, 500,000 bushels; wheat, 40,000 bushels; oats, 110,000 bushels; sweet potatoes, 35,000 bushels; cotton, 4,000,000 pounds; wool, 12,000 pounds.

Stock: horses and mules, 3,012; cattle, 11,452; sheep, 8,171; hogs, 23,000.

Natural forest: oak, pine, walnut and hickory.

Rivers: Rocky and Yadkin. Creeks: Brown's, Lane's, Guild's and Jones. Mills, 20; tanneries, 2; distilleries, 20; spirits manufactured, 1,500 gallons. Gold mine, Bailey's.

Churches, 23; College, Carolina Female. Academies; Blanch's, Gum Spring, Lilesville, and Rocky Hill. Schools abundant.

Soil fertile, surface unbroken. Cotton grows finely and is the chief market crop. People intelligent and many substantial planters.

The Wilmington, Charlotte and Rutherfordton Rail Road passes through the county.

WADESBORO', the county seat, is about 120 miles south-west from Raleigh.

ASHE.

This county, named in honor of Gov. Ashe, was formed in 1799. Population, 7,000.

Farms, 750; acres improved, 50,000; acres unimproved, 145,000.

Annual products: corn, 110,000 bushels; wheat, 3,500 do;

oats, 100,000 do; pease, 1,500 do; buckwheat, 5,000 do; Irish potatoes, 2,500 do; butter, 95,000 pounds; maple sugar, 10,-815 do; tobacco, 5,000 do; wool, 10,500 do; honey and beeswax, 18,000 do; flax, 15,500 do; hay 5,000 tons.

Stock: horses and mules, 1,500; cattle, 6,500; sheep, 4,500; hogs, 14,000.

Forest: oak, hickory, maple, ash and walnut.

Surface, mountainous. Soil, on hill sides and valleys, very productive. Climate, healthy. This county is at present without railroad facilities; therefore land is cheap. A fine grazing region.

Jefferson the county seat, is about 200 miles northwest of Raleigh.

BEAUFORT.

This county, named for the Duke of Beaufort, lies in the Eastern part of the State. It was organized in 1741.

Area, 600 square miles.

Population, 12,500.

Soil, very fertile.

Farms, 594; acres improved, 30,760; acres unimproved, 180,981.

Annual products: corn, 160,000 bushels; wheat, 7,000 bushels; oats, 6,000 bushels; Irish and sweet potatoes, 160,000 bushels; pease, 20,000 bushels; cotton, 1,000,000 pounds; tar, pitch and turpentine, 110,000 barrels; fish, 5,000 barrels; lumber, very large quantities.

Stock: horses and mules, 1,150; cattle, 13,500; sheep, 8,250; hogs, 18,279.

Trees, natural: cypress, juniper, long-leaf pine, oak, hickory and gum.

There are in this county large tracts of swamp or poccosin lands, which, when cleared and cultivated, will produce from 50 to 100 bushels of corn, or from 400 to 500 pounds of lint cotton per acre. They may be had very cheap and offer great inducements to actual settlers.

Washington, the county seat, lies at the head of the Pamplico river, and is 120 miles east by south from Raleigh. Population, about 2,000. It carries on a large export trade with New York and the West Indies. Other towns are Aurora and Bath.

BERTIE.

This county, which lies on the Albemarle Sound and between he Chowan and Roanoke rivers, was organized in 1733.

Area, 800 square miles.

Population, 13,000.

Doctors, 6; lawyers, 5; churches, 17; post offices, 6; mills, many; distilleries, (turpentine,) several.

Farms, 524; acres improved, 92,600; acres unimproved, 203,803.

Annual products: corn, 560,000 bushels; wheat, 3,000 bushels; sweet potatoes, 100,000 bushels; pease, 90,000 bushels; cotton, 2,200,000 pounds; wool 12,000 pounds; fish, 25,000 barrels; hay, 35,000 tons.

Stock: horses and mules, 2,297; cattle, 10,880; sheep, 6,654; hogs, 33,081.

Native growth: long-leaf pine, juniper, cypress, oak and hickory. Pine and cypress timber valuable.

Rivers: Roanoke, Chowan, Cashie and Cashoke.

This county abounds in rich lands, of which the best are still covered with dense forest, offering great inducements to lumbermen. Fruits and vegetables grow here a month earlier than in New Jersey, and may be transported directly by water from the farm to New York.

The fisheries of this county are sources of great profit.

Cotton grows finely in Bertie.

WINDSOR, the county seat, situated on the Cashie river, is 157 miles east from Raleigh.

BLADEN.

This county, which lies in the South-eastern part of the State, was formed in 1734.

Area, 800 square miles.

Population, 10,000.

Doctors, 9; lawyers, 4; churches, 25; schools, number not known; mills, saw, 6; distilleries, turpentine, 6; manufactories, turpentine and tar, 40.

Farms, 486; acres, improved, 47,608; acres, unimproved, 400,000.

Annual products: corn, 200,000 bushels; wheat, 15,000 bushels; oats, 5,000 bushels; sweet potatoes, 100,000 bushels; cotton, 60,000 pounds; wool, 7,500 pounds; rice, 75,000 pounds; pease, large quantities; turpentine, 15,000 barrels; lumber, value, $50,000.

This is a very fertile county, capable of great development; and when its rich swamp lands are drained and cultivated, will produce ten fold more than it does at present Lands cheap. The Wilmington, Charlotte and Ruth. Rail Road runs through it, and furnishes, in connection with its rivers and creeks, easy transportation to a good market at Wilmington.

ELIZABETH TOWN, the county seat is situated on Cape Fear river, and is 60 miles from Wilmington, and about 90 miles Southeast from Raleigh.

BRUNSWICK.

This county, which lies in the extreme Southeastern part of the State, was organized in 1764. Surface, level. Soil, sandy.

Area, 950 square miles.

Population, 8,000.

Lawyers, 4; churches, 23; post offices, 4; Academies, Wayman and Smithville; Schools convenient; manufactories, tar and turpentine, 50.

Farms, 385; acres improved, 18,500; acres unimproved, 247,600.

Annual products: corn, 60,000 bushels; sweet potatoes, 118,000 bushels; cotton, 10,000 pounds; wool, 3,000 pounds; rice, 3,000,000 pounds; lumber, value, $15,000; tar, pitch and turpentine, value $18,000; machines, rice, 6.

Stock: horses and mules, 1,000; cattle, 8,500; sheep, 3,500; hogs, 12,525.

Trees, natural: long-leaf pine, juniper, live oak and cypress.

Green and Cypress Swamps abound in timber, and when cleared, ditched and cultivated, will yield most abundant crops.

200,000 acres of the best lands are for sale, and offer splendid openings for capital, labor and skill.

SMITHVILLE, the county seat, situated on the Elizabeth river, near the mouth of the Cape Fear river, in sight of the ocean, is 173 miles South-west of Raleigh. It is a place of fashionable summer resort. In the vicinity are Forts Johnson and Caswell.

BUNCOMBE.

This county, named for Col. Buncombe of Washington county, was organized in 1791.

Area, 5,000 square miles.

Population, 13,000.

Ministers, 15; doctors, 14; lawyers, 19; churches, 20; mills, grist, 15; factories, &c., 6; newspapers, 2; post offices, 9.

Farms, 1,250; acres, improved, 75,350; acres unimproved, 506,200.

Annual products: corn, 50,000 bushels; wheat, 25,000 bushels; oats and rye, 150,000 bushels; butter, 125,000 pounds; wool, 150,000 pounds; tobacco, 10,000; ginseng, value, $18,000; apples, peaches, Irish potatoes, &c., large quantities.

Stock: horses and mules, 3,708; cattle, 16,500; sheep, 14,000; hogs, 28,608.

Native forest: hickory, oak, maple, ash and walnut.

This county lies amid the ranges of the Blue Ridge, and is watered by the Swannanoa and French Broad Rivers, and by numerous creeks and mountain streams. It is one of the most salubrious portions of this continent. Mineral springs of great value abound. The soil, in the valleys and mountain sides, is very productive. Fruits and vegetables grow luxuriantly. Apples weighing from 14 to 15 ounces are common. Lands vary from one dollar to fifty dollars per acre.

ASHEVILLE, the county seat, is 250 miles from Raleigh. It is much visited by invalids from various parts of the State.

The proposed route of the Western North Carolina Rail Road, which will connect Beaufort Harbor on the Atlantic ocean, with Tennessee, runs near Asheville, and, when completed, will make it accessible to all portions of the land.

BURKE.

This county, named for Sir Edmund Burke, the great English orator, was founded in 1777.

Area, 400 square miles.

Population 10,000.

Doctors, 7; lawyers, 4; churches, 28; mills, 12; post offices, 4; schools, Morganton Academy, Rock Seminary, &c.

Farms, 375 ; acres improved, 30,000; acres unimproved, 110,000.

Annual products: corn, 600,000 bushels; wheat, 45,000 bushels; oats and rye, 36,000 bushels; cotton, 50,000 pounds; wool, 26,000 pounds; tobacco, 18,000 pounds.

Gold, in 1850, value, $50,000.

Stock: horses and mules, 1,550; cattle, 5,250; sheep, 3,528; hogs, 10,660.

Trees, natural: hickory, oak, walnut, &c.

This county lies on the Eastern side of the Blue Ridge, and is watered by the Catawba, Sumerville and John's Rivers, and numerous creeks. Surface, broken and hilly. Soil, rich and productive. Scenery, charming. Climate, most salubrious. The Western North Carolina Rail Road runs through this county.

MORGANTON, the county seat, is 1,100 feet above the level of the sea, and lies 197 miles west from Raleigh. It is a place of resort in summer, for pleasure seekers and invalids.

CABARRUS.

This county lies in the southwestern part of the State. It was formed out of Mecklenburg in 1802.

Area, 350 square miles.

Population 10,450.

Ministers, 15; doctors, 12; Lawyers, 4; churches, 23; cotton factories, 2; grist mills, 15; tanneries, 6; North Carolina college at Mount Pleasant; Classical school at Concord, and others. Gold and copper mines, 7.

The Reed Gold Mine was discovered in 1799 and is said to have been the first discovered in the United States. Several of these mines have been very productive.

Farms, 845: acres improved, 64,500; unimproved, 125,700.

Annual products: corn, 500,000 bushels; wheat, 85,000 bushels; oats and rye, 56,000 bushels; sweat potatoes, 25,000 bushels; cotton, 1,000,000 pounds; wool, 16,000 pounds.

Stock: horses and mules, 3,500; cattle, 4,500; sheep, 5,000 hogs, 10,550.

Trees, natural: poplar, oak, walnut, hickory, &c.

Soil fertile. Population, intelligent and moral.

CONCORD, the county seat, contains about 1800 inhabitants, and is 139 miles from Raleigh.

CALDWELL.

This county, named after Pres. Caldwell of Chapel Hill, was organized in 1841. It lies in the mountains.

Area, 450 square miles.

Population 4,500.

Ministers, 19; Doctors, 4; churches, 20; schools: Davenport Female College at Lenoir; Lenoir Male Academy; Mount Bethel Academy and others.

Farms, 366; acres improved, 25,500; unimproved, 100,000.

Annual products: corn, 200,000 bushels; wheat, 5,000 bushels; oats and rye, 35,000 bushels; Irish potatoes, 15,000 bushels; peas, 2,000 bushels; butter, 40,000 pounds.

Stock: horses and mules, 1,226; cattle, 4,500; sheep, 4,225; hogs, 11,225.

Forest: oak, hickory, walnut, maple, &c.

This county is watered by the Catawba, Yadkin and John's rivers and by Buffalo and King's creeks.

The county is mountainous. The farming lands are rich and productive. It contains a most excellent population.

Lenoir, the county seat, is 200 miles west of Raleigh. A favorite resort in summer.

CAMDEN.

This county, named after Earl Camden of England, was organized in 1777. It lies in the north-eastern part of the

State. Surface, level. Soil, generally a sandy loam and very rich and fertile.

Area, 280 square miles.

Population, 1,500.

Ministers, 6; lawyers, 6; doctors, 3; churches, 8; post offices, 2; mills, 3; schools: Jonesboro and Savage Creek Academies; shingle mills, 6.

Farms, 579: acres improved, 38,400; unimproved, 36,950.

Annual products: corn, 360,000 bushels; wheat, 3,500 bushels; oats and rye, 10,000 bushels; peas, 10,000 bushels; sweet potatoes, 39,000 bushels; cotton, 10,000 pounds; wool 5,000 pounds; flax, 36,000 pounds; honey and beeswax, 10,500 pounds; fish, 1,000 barrels; lumber, value, $15,000; brandy, value, $2,500.

This county is peculiarly adapted to the culture of early fruits and vegetables, which find a profitable market at Baltimore, Philadelphia and New York, *via* Norfolk, Va., by the Dismal Swamp canal.

CAMDEN COURT HOUSE, the county seat, is 219 miles northeast from Raleigh.

CARTERET.

This county was one of the original English settlements. It lies on the Atlantic coast.

Area, ... square miles.

Population 8,000.

Ministers, 6; doctors, 10; lawyers, 4; churches, 7; post offices, 3; manufactories, 2.

Farms, 394; acres improved, 30,769; unimproved, 180,981.

Annual products: corn, 52,500 bushels; wheat, 3,000 bushels; oats, 1,000 bushels; rye, 1,000 bushels; pease, 55,000 bushels, wool, 3,000 pounds; butter, 2,000 pounds; honey, 6,000 pounds; hay, 500 tons.

Stock: horses and mules, 1,120; cattle, 13,980; sheep, 8,169; hogs, 18,279.

Trees: long-leaf pine, oak, hickory, persimmon and cedar.

The Atlantic Rail Road runs through this county, connecting Morehead City with Goldsboro, the Eastern terminus of the North Carolina Rail Road.

There is a large quantity of swamp land in the county belonging to the State, which will soon be brought into market.

BEAUFORT, the county seat, distant 150 miles from Raleigh, has a very fine harbor, and is a fashionable summer resort.

CASWELL.

This county, named after the first Governor of North Carolina, was formed from Orange county in 1777.

Area, 400 square miles.

Population, 16,500.

Surface, hilly. Soil, good and productive. Tobacco and wheat are the principal market crops.

Ministers, 12; doctors, 15; lawyers, 5; churches, 25; schools, Dan River Institute, Leasburg male and female, and Milton female academies, and others. Post offices, 8; mills, grist, 24; foundry, 1; cotton factory.

Farms, 735; acres improved, 123,000; unimproved, 115,890.

Annual products: corn, 360,000 bushels; wheat, 12,100 bushels; oats, 3,000 bushels; rye, 3,000 bushels; sweet potatoes, 32,000; pease, 3,000 bushels; cotton, 100,000 pounds; wool, 8,500 pounds; butter, 75,000 pounds; tobacco, 3,550,-000 pounds; flax, 8,000 pounds; honey and beeswax, 12,500 pounds; hay, 3,000 tons.

Stock: horses and mules, 2,500; cattle, 7,000; sheep, 7,500; hogs, 21,225.

Forests: oak, pine, hickory, gum and ash.

The Greenboro and Danville Va., Rail Road runs through the Northwest part of the county. Land from $2 to $10 per acre.

YANCEYVILLE, the county seat, is 66 miles Northwest from Raleigh.

CATAWBA.

This county, named from the Catawba river, was formed from Lincoln county, in 1842.

Area 250 square miles.

Population, 11,000.

Surface, hilly.

Soil, rich.

Ministers, 8; doctors 3; lawyers 3; churches, 30; post offices, 6; iron forges, 2; foundries, 4.

Farms, 939; acres improved, 64,500; unimproved, 154,225.

Annual products: corn, 350,000 bushels; wheat, 50,000 bushels; oats and rye, 65,000 bushels; Irish and sweet potatoes, 35,000 bushels; butter, 75,000 pounds; wool, 10,500 pounds; flax, 7,000 pounds; tobacco, 6,500 pounds; honey and beeswax, 11,250 pounds; hay, 3,000 tons.

Stock: horses and mules, 2,915; cattle, 6,115; sheep, 6,250; hogs, 20,000.

Trees, natural: maple, walnut, hickory, oak.

The Western N. C. Rail Road runs through the length of this county. Iron ore abundant. Lands cheap.

NEWTON, the county seat, is 175 miles west from Raleigh.

CHATHAM.

This county was organized in 1770, named after Earl Chatham of England. Surface very broken, soil fertile.

Area, 700 square miles.

Population, 28,000.

Farms, 1,635; 139,500 acres improved; 300,000 acres unimproved.

Annual Productions about 650,000 bushels corn; 125,000 bushels wheat; 100,000 bushels oats; 500,000 pounds tobacco; 5,000 tons of hay; 1,000 bales of cotton; 10,000 pounds of iron; $5,000 worth of lumber; 90,000 bushels sweet and Irish potatoes; 150,000 pounds of butter and cheese; 15,500 bushels pease; 10,000 pounds flax; 10,000 pounds wool; 5,000 pounds honey and beeswax.

Churches, 50; ministers, 23; doctors, 15; lawyers, 7.

Factories, &c: Egypt mining company's foundery and machine shop at Lockville; iron manufacturing company at Egypt; grist mills, 25; post offices, 13.

Schools: Pittsboro' scientific academy; Pittsboro' female academy; Haywood high school; Mt. Vernon seminary.

The Chatham Coal Fields in this county are generally known. A Rail Road has been completed from Fayetteville to the Coal Fields, on Deep river. Another Rail Road is being pushed through from Carey, on the North Carolina Central Rail Road, eight miles from Raleigh to Columbia, S. C.; besides these, other Roads are projected, which must fully develope this mineral region.

These improvements will make Chatham one of the most prosperous counties in the State. 300,000 acres of good lands in this county will be brought into market. Lands are now cheap.

Forests: Oak, hickory, maple, walnut and pine.

Pittsboro' is the county seat.

CHEROKEE.

This county was organized in 1839 from Macon, derives its name from a tribe of Indians, some of whom still remain. It lies in the extreme south-western part of the State. The face of the county is mountainous and picturesque.

Area 700 square miles.

Population 6,000.

Forests: maple, oak, hickory, ash, walnut, &c.

2

Farms 450; 25,000 acres improved; 75,000 unimproved.

Annual productions about, 205,000 bushels of corn; 3,000 bushels of wheat; 35,000 bushels of oats; 2,000 bushels of rye; 25,000 bushels of sweet potatoes; 50,000 pounds of butter and cheese.

Stock: 1,500 horses and mules; 6,500 cattle; 5,000 sheep; 12,000 hogs.

Gold and iron are found.

Churches 10; ministers 6; lawyers 2; doctors 4; grist mills 10; merchants 10; post offices 4.

This county is watered by the Hiawassee, Valley and Notley rivers and a number of mountain streams.

Its mines of flesh colored marble, gold, copper, iron and silver, are to be developed at a future day, when rail roads penetrate the mountains.

The soil is very rich in the valleys and along the streams. Land is very cheap and abundant. A fine grazing county.

MURPHY is the county seat, it lies near the junction of Hiawassee and Valley rivers, on the route of the Western Turnpike.

CHOWAN.

This county derived its charter from King Charles the II, and its name from an Indian tribe. It lies in the Northeastern part of the State and is watered by the Albemarle Sound and Chowan River.

Area 250 square miles.

Farms: 344; 40,000 acres improved; 52,000 unimproved.

Stock: horses and mules, 1,200; cattle, 4,500; sheep, 2,500; hogs, 15,000.

Annual products about 300,000 bushels of corn; 20,000 bushels wheat; 15,000 bushels oats; 150,000 pounds cotton; 20,000 barrels of fish; 95,000 bushels sweet potatoes; 35,000 bushels pease; 15,000 pounds butter and cheese; 1,670 tons of hay; 10,500 pounds rice.

Churches 20; lawyers 5; doctors 7; grist mills 4.

Academies: Edenton academy, Episcopal parochial school, and several others; postoffices, 3.

It was from this county the first bag of cotton was shipped in July 1768.

The Albemarle Sound Fisheries are large and very profitable. Some of the seines are drawn by mules and windlass, and are said to be two miles in length. The quantity of shad, herring, rock and other fish caught in these waters is immense.

This county possesses great water facilities. Sail vessels and steamboats navigate the Sound and rivers. A Rail Road is projected from Edenton to Suffolk, Va. The winters are mild, stock need but little wintering and can be raised in large quantities.

Timber: pitch pine, gum, oak, cypress, juniper and cedar.

The lands are fertile, and produce corn, wheat and cotton finely.

EDENTON, the county seat, settled in 1716, and has been the abode of wealth and refinement. Distance from Raleigh 150 miles.

CLAY.

This county was lately organized from the southern part of Cherokee.

Area, 250 square miles.

Population, 3,000.

Annual products: corn, 50,000 bushels; wheat, 1,000 bushels; Irish potatoes, 10,000 bushels; Mines: gold, silver, copper and iron.

Natural growth of timber: oak, hickory, chesnut, &c.

Lands abundant and cheap. A fine grazing region.

FORT HEMBRIE, the county seat, is 360 miles west from Raleigh.

CLEAVELAND.

This county was organized out of Lincoln and Rutherford in 1840.

Area, 650 square miles.

Population, 12,500.

Doctors, 6; lawyers, 4; churches, 30; mills: grist, 10; saw, 4; paper, 1; Tanneries, 5; Iron forges, 3.

Farms, 961; acres improved, 62,000; unimproved, 186,500.

Annual products: corn, 450,000 bushels; wheat, 36,000 bushels; oats and rye, 65,000 bushels; pease, 5,000 bushels; butter and cheese, 100,000 pounds; cotton, 200,000 pounds; wool, 15,000 pounds; flax, 2,000 pounds; tobacco, 6,000 pounds; honey and beeswax, 10,000 pounds.

Stock: horses and mules, 3,500; cattle, 7,500; sheep, 8,000; hogs, 16,500.

Native growth: pine, chestnut, oak, hickory, &c.

SHELBY, the county seat, is 190 miles south by west from Raleigh.

The Wilmington, Charlotte and Rutherford Railroad runs through this county.

COLUMBUS.

Was organized in 1808 and named after Columbus, the great discoverer.

Surface, level; soil sandy on the ridges, rich, near and on the water courses. It is drained by the Waccamaw, and Lumber rivers, White Gum and Beaver creeks.

Area, 600 square miles.

Population, 9,000.

Annual products: 2,000 bushels wheat; 200,000 bushels corn; 5,000 bushels oats and rye; 200,000 bushels sweet potatoes; 5,000 bushels peas; 16,000 pounds butter and cheese; 2,000 barrels turpentine; $20,000 worth of lumber; 50,000 pounds cotton; 8,000 pounds wool.

Farms, 400 ; 26,000 acres improved; 262,000 acres unimproved.

Stock: 750 horses and mules; 10,600 cattle; 14,500 sheep; hogs, 20,000.

Churches 20; lawyers, 4; doctors, 4.

Schools: Whitesville academy and other schools.

Timber: long-leaf pine, white oak, red oak, Spanish oak, water oak, juniper, cypress, &c.

This county is one whose prospective wealth is difficult to estimate. Its resources, extensive forests and rich soil with facilities for transportation by water and rail road are excelled by few counties in the State. The Manchester and Wilmington rail road runs through this county. Marl of the best kind for manure is found in nearly all parts of this county. 300,000 acres of splendid timber and farming lands are in the market, from one dollar to five dollars per acre. The far-famed Scuppernong grape grows here finely, and the native wines made are of the best kind. The business of making wine is profitable and increasing.

WHITEVILLE is the county town. It is near the Wilming- and Manchester rail road, about 50 miles from Wilmington and 150 miles from Raleigh.

CRAVEN.

This county was settled and organized in 1729.

Area, land and water, 1,000 square miles.

Population, 16,500.

Doctors, 20; lawyers, 10; churches, 25; post offices, 6. Mills: grist, 6; saw, 4; shingle, 4. Manufactories, tar and turpentine, 40. Schools, 12.

Farms, 400; acres improved, 63,450; unimproved, 300,000; cash value of farms, $1,375,500.

Annual products: corn, 314,000 bushels; wheat, 4,540 bushels; rye, 3,500 bushels; oats, 3,000 bushels; pease, 30,000 bushels; Irish potatoes, 9,550 bushels; sweet potatoes, 150,000 bushels; butter, 21,000 pounds; rice, 35,000 pounds; wool, 10,834 pounds; honey, 52,000 pounds; beeswax, 5,000 pounds; turpentine, 150,000 barrels; fish, 25,000 barrels; hay, 1,375 tons; fruits, value, $5,000; lumber, value, $50,000.

Stock: horses and mules, 1,400; cattle, 13,772; sheep, 6,037; hogs, 25,000.

Trees, natural: pitch pine, white and red oak, juniper and cypress.

Soil, on streams and lakes, rich and valuable. Marl of the best kind abundant. The soil and climate are admirably adapted to the culture of grapes of all kinds.

NEW BERNE, the county seat, derived its name from Berne, in Switzerland, whence Baron de Graffenreidt emigrated in 1709, being followed the second year by 1,500. It is situated at the junction of the Trent and Neuse rivers, is a port of entry and carries on considerable trade. It is 120 miles from Raleigh.

CUMBERLAND.

This county, named in honor of the Duke of Cumberland was organized in 1764. It lies in the Southern part of the State.

Area, 600 square miles.

Population, 15,500.

Ministers, 25; lawyers, 16; doctors, 19; churches, 32; schools: Academies, 6, and other schools. Mills, cotton, 3; grist, 10; distilleries, turpentine, 23; post offices, 8.

Farms, 1,000; acres improved, 63,500; unimproved, 300,000.

Annual products: corn, 313,413 bushels; wheat, 4,500 bushels; rye, 3,500 bushels; oats, 2,619 bushels; pease and beans, 29,549 bushels; Irish potatoes, 9,575 bushels; sweet potatoes, 150,000 bushels; butter, 25,000 pounds; rice, 32,000 pounds; wool, 10,957 pounds; cotton, 400,000 pounds, honey, 6,500 pounds; hay, 2,625 tons; wine, 1,550 gallons.

Stock: horses and mules, 1,500; cattle, 13,015; sheep, 6,007.

Trees, natural: oak, pine, gum, ash, poplar, cypress, &c.

This county is watered by the Cape Fear and Lower Little rivers and their tributaries. The Cape Fear is navigable to Fayetteville. The water power in this county is immense, and if controlled by scientific and energetic men, would become a source of great wealth. Capitalists and manufacturers should visit and examine this most valuable portion of the State with the view of investment.

FAYETTEVILLE, the county seat, is one of the largest cities in the State. It is 100 miles by water from Wilmington and 60 miles from Raleigh. Its location, and natural and artificial resources promise for it a future of great material prosperity.

CURRITUCK.

This county, named from an Indian tribe, lies in the northeastern part of the State.

Area, 200 square miles.

Population, 7,500.

Doctors, 6; lawyers, 3; churches, 12; academies, 2 and other schools; post offices, 3.

Farms, 500: acres improved, 37,000; unimproved, 90,000.

Annual products: corn, 300,000 bushels; wheat, 1,500 bushels; oats and rye 2,860 bushels; peas, 40,000 bushels; Irish and sweet potatoes, 150,000 bushels; butter, 54,000 pounds; flax, 30,000 pounds; wool, 12,500 pounds; beeswax and honey, 5,000 pounds; scuppernong and other grapes grow finely.

Lands generally good and productive—recovered swamp lands very rich. Fine fishing section and immense quantities of wild game.

Stock: horses and mules, 1,085; cattle, 7,250; sheep, 6,000; hogs, 15,500.

Forests: oak, pine, juniper and cypress.

CURRITUCK COURT HOUSE, the county seat, 240 miles from Raleigh.

DAVIDSON.

This county was organized from Rowan in 1822.

Area, 650 square miles.

Population 16,000.

Surface, hilly. Lands productive. On the rivers very fine. The " Jersey settlement" is a splendid farming section.

Doctors, 12; lawyers, 8; churches, 41; colleges, 3, and other schools; post offices, 6; factories, 3; mills, grist, 15; Mines: gold, silver, lead and copper.

Farms, 1,250: acres improved, 121,500; unimproved, 200,000; farms, value, $1,988,000.

Annual products: corn, 500,000 bushels; wheat, 225,000 bushels; rye, 2,000 bushels; oats, 100,000 bushels; peas, 10,000 bushels; Irish and sweet potatoes, 51,750 bushels; butter, 85,000 pounds; cotton, 280,000 pounds; wool, 20,000 pounds; flax, 5,500 pounds; tobacco, 125,000 pounds; rice, 15,000 pounds; honey, 50,000 pounds; hay, 3,000 tons; sorghum, 10,000 gallons; fruits, value $28,000.

Stock: horses and mules, 4,000; cattle, 9,133; hogs, 28,105.

Trees, natural: ash, oak, elm,, hickory, poplar, chesnut, &c.

Several farms in this county highly improved.

LEXINGTON, the county seat, is 117 miles west of Raleigh on the North Carolina Rail Road.

DAVIE.

This county was taken from Rowan county, 1836.

Area, 250 square miles.

Population, 8,500.

Doctors, 14; lawyers, 2; churches, 18; academies, 4; post offices, 6; grist mills, 17; tobacco factories, 5; distilleries, 18, tanneries, 4.

Farms, 410: acres improved, 60,000; unimproved, 95,000; value, $1,335,000.

Annual products: corn, 320,000 bushels; wheat, 105,000 bushels; oats, 64,000 bushels; rye, 3,900 bushels; peas, 8,500 bushels; Irish potatoes, 6,000 bushels; sweet potatoes, 14,000 bushels; butter, 45,000 pounds; honey, 1,700 pounds; wool, 7,500 pounds; tobacco, 400,000 pounds; hay, 4,000 tons; Sorghum, 4,000 gallons; fruits, value $10,000.

Stock: horses and mules, 2,000; cattle, 4,797; sheep, 5,110; hogs, 1,370.

Trees, natural: ash, elm, hickory, oak, &c.

The lands are generally good, and well adapted to improved culture. Prices moderate.

MOCKSVILLE, the county seat, is 135 miles from Raleigh.

DUPLIN.

This county was organized in 1749.

Area, 670 square miles.

Population, 15,800.

Doctors, 12; lawyers, 6; churches, 20; academies, 4; post offices 6; saw-mills, 12; tar and turpentine factories, 20.

Farms, 923; acres improved, 107,000; unimproved, 340,000; value, $3,132,000.

Annual products: corn, 425,000 bushels; wheat, 5,000 bushels; oats, 4,000 bushels; rye, 6,852 bushels; pease, 65,000 bushels; Irish potatoes, 10,000 bushels; sweet potatoes, 305,000 bushels, butter, 60,000 pounds; cotton, 8,000,000 pounds; wool, 13,000 pounds; rice, 125,000 pounds; honey, 51,554 pounds; beeswax, 4,000 pounds; hay, 2,860 tons; fruits, value $2,500.

Stock: horses and mules, 2,500; cattle, 11,250; sheep, 4,500; hogs, 39,000.

Trees, natural: oak, hickory, pine, &c.

Soil sandy but productive. Improved swamp lands very fine. Markets easy of access. Wilmington and Weldon Rail Road runs through the county.

KENANSVILLE, the county seat, is 86 miles from Raleigh.

EDGECOMBE.

This county was organized, from Craven, in 1733.

Area, 600 square miles.

Soil good. Muck and marl abundant.

Population, 17,300.

Farms, 900; acres improved, 134,758; unimproved, 174,600; value $4,974,920.

Doctors, 25; lawyers, 7; churches, 23; schools, 15; grist mills, 7; cotton factory, 1.

Annual products: corn, 725,500 bushels; wheat, 12,500 bushels; rye, 11,000 bushels; oats, 66,225 bushels; pease, 97,758, bushels; Irish potatoes, 15,250 bushels; sweet potatoes, 200,000 bushels; butter, 32,000 pounds; cotton, 10,000,000 pounds; wool, 9,452 pounds; rice, 6,000 pounds; beeswax, 2,721 pounds; honey, 2,500 pounds; wine, 2,500 gallons; hay, 5,408 tons; fruits, value $12,000.

Stock: horses and mules, 4,000; cattle, 9,790; sheep, 5,250; hogs, 50,000.

This is the most highly improved agricultural county in the State. Edgecombe is the banner cotton county in the State. Accessible to market by Rail Road and water communication.

TARBORO, the county seat, situated on Tar river is 76 miles East from Raleigh.

FORSYTHE.

This county was organized out of Stokes in 1848.

Area, 250 square miles.

Population 12,000.

Farms, 1,000; acres improved, 75,000; unimproved, 132,-500; cash value, $1,175,800.

Annual products: corn, 318,000 bushels; wheat, 188,000 bushels; oats, 60,950 bushels; rye, 8,132 bushels; Irish potatoes, 12,000 bushels; sweet potatoes, 21,000 bushels, pease, 2,350 bushels; butter, 75,000 pounds; honey, 47,000; wool, 10,000 pounds; tobacco, 552,000 pounds; flax seed, 5,586 bushels; hay, 5,500 tons; fruit, value, $35,000.

Stock: horses, 2,275; mules, 300; cattle, 6,134; sheep, 6,386; hogs, 19,000.

Churches, 24; schools, 12; mills, grist, 25; saw, 6; paper, 1; factories, cotton, 1; woolen, 1; post offices, 7; ministers, 15; lawyers, 6; doctors, 14.

This county is peculiarly adapted to fruit, grain and grass.

WINSTON is the county seat.

Salem, contiguous to Winston, is a beautiful village, founded by the Moravians. The Female School at this place has been in successful operation for more than half a century, and is justly celebrated. More Southern women have been educated here than at any other school in the country.

FRANKLIN.

This county, named after Benjamin Franklin, was organized in 1779.

Area, 450 square miles.

Population, 14,100.

Farms, 650; acres improved, 119,000; unimproved, 150,000; cash value, $3,500,000.

Annual products: corn, 416,500 bushels; wheat, 45,000 bushels; oats, 32,000 bushels; rye, 11,300 bushels; Irish potatoes, 8,250 bushels; sweet potatoes, 11,000 bushels; pease, 32,634 bushels; cotton, 990,000 pounds; wool, 8,500 pounds; tobacco, 1,962,385 pounds; butter, 70,000 pounds; honey, 20,000 pounds; hay, 13,000 tons; fruits, value, $10,000.

Stock: horses and mules, 2,500; cattle, 8,675; sheep, 6,250; hogs, 27,250.

Forests: ash, elm, oak, hickory and gum.

Churches, 26; schools, 5; mills: grist, 75; saw, 10; tanneries, 14; post offices, 6; doctors, 15; lawyers, 6.

The lands are well adapted to cotton culture. It is a healthy section, people intelligent and hospitable.

LOUISBURG, the county seat, on the Tar river, is 35 miles from Raleigh. There is a Female College and an excellent male Academy in this place.

The Raleigh & Gaston Rail Road runs through this county.

GASTON.

This county, named for Judge Gaston, was organized in 1846.

Area, 350 square miles.

Population, 9500.

Farms, 825; acres improved, 52,800; unimproved 167,500. Cash value 1,529,225.

Annual products: corn, 344,000 bushels; wheat, 74,000 bushels; oats, 17,000 bushels; pease, 8,000 bushels; Irish potatoes, 5,000 bushels; sweet potatoes, 21,000 bushels; butter, 85,500 pounds; wool, 10,500 pounds; tobacco, 5,000 pounds, honey, 20,500 pounds; hay, 1,250 tons; sorghum, 4,250 gallons; fruits, value $5,600.

Stock: horses and mules, 2,500; cattle, 6,195; sheep, 5,366; hogs, 15,335.

Trees, natural: ash, hickory, white and red oak, elm and walnut.

Doctors, 8; lawyers, 2; churches, 20; postoffices, 10. Mines, gold, 4. Mills, cotton, 3; grist, 14. Factories, 2.

It is watered by the Catawba and its tributaries. Lands are good and well adapted to wheat, corn and the grasses. Gold mines have been opened here. Water power abundant.

DALLAS, a small village, is the county seat.

GATES.

This county, named after General Gates, was organized in 1779.

Area, 300 square miles.

Population, 8,444.

Farms, 525; acres, improved, 72,678; unimproved, 83,673. Cash value, $950,000.

Annual products: corn; 420,693 bushels; wheat, 10,000 bushels; oats, 6,852 bushels; rye, 1,435 bushels; pease, 44,828 bushels; Irish potatoes, 8,684 bushels; sweet potatoes, 162,000 bushels; butter, 15,000 pounds; wool, 5,000 pounds; tobacco, 2,000 pounds; honey, 6,000 pounds; hay, 2,800 tons: fruits, value, $5,000.

Stock: horses, 1,147; mules, 250; cattle, 6,500; sheep, 2,817; hogs, 25,833.

Trees, natural: pine, oak, (white, Spanish, and red.) hickory, juniper, cypress and gum.

Doctors, 7; lawyers, 2; churches, 17; academies, 10; post offices, 6; factories, 6; mills, grist, 8; shingle, 6

The oak and cypress timber of this county is valuable. Soil good and adapted to corn, wheat, cotton and fruits. Recovered swamp lands very good.

GATESVILLE, the county seat is 155 miles North-east from Raleigh.

GRANVILLE.

This county was formed from Edgecombe in 1786.

Area, 750 square miles.

Population, 24,396.

Soil good, red, yellow and gray.

Farms: 1,250; acres improved, 197,500; unimproved, 245,-500. Cash value, $3,500,000.

Annual products: corn, 349,777 bushels; wheat, 183,550 bushels; oats, 150,000 bushels; rye, 322 bushels; pease, 8,000 bushels; Irish potatoes, 12,800 bushels; sweet potatoes, 93,-800 bushels; butter, 110,000 pounds; honey, 20,000 pounds; wool, 20,500; tobacco, 6,625,594 pounds; hay, 15,000 tons; fruits, value, $3,000.

Stock: horses, 4,294; mules, 500; cattle, 10,500; sheep, 15,810; hogs, 34,249.

Trees, natural: oak, (white, Spanish, red and chestnut) hickory, ash, elm and gum. Lands productive in wheat, tobacco and corn.

Churches, 50; schools, 18; mills, grist, 13; factories, tobacco, 6; iron, 1; tanneries, 6; post offices, 10; doctors, 20; lawyers, 19.

OXFORD, the county seat, a beautiful village, is 45 miles from Raleigh. The Raleigh & Gaston Rail Road runs through this county.

Henderson, located on the Raleigh & Gaston Rail Road is a growing place, and well situated for trade in a good farming section.

GREENE.

This county was organized, as Dobbs county, in 1779. The name was changed to Greene county in 1799.

Area, 280 square miles.

Population 7,935.

Farms, 5000: acres improved, 63,500; unimproved, 87,500. Cash value, $1,658,998.

Annual products: corn 312,820 bushels; wheat 10,757 bushels; oats 6,020 bushels; rye 8,650 bushels; pease 65,000 bushels; Irish potatoes 7,750 bushels; sweet potatoes 76,458 bushels; butter 15,000 pounds; cotton 1,835,600 pounds; wool 3,335 pounds; rice 6,500 pounds; honey 12,000 pounds; hay 3,500 tons; wine 1,100 gallons; fruits, value $3,000.

Stock: horses 1,000; mules 500; cattle 3,068; sheep 2,053; hogs 22,000.

Forest: oaks, ash, elm, hickory and pine.

Doctors, 6; lawyers, 2; churches, 15; academics, 4; and other schools in the county. Mills, grist 5.

Marl of fine quality is found in this connty. Land productive. Cotton and corn grow well. The grape grows finely.

SNOW HILL the county seat, is 70 miles east from Raleigh.

GUILFORD.

This county was organized from Rowan and Orange counties in 1770.

Area, 600 square miles.

Population, 20,500.

Surface level, soil good.

Farms, 1,500: acres improved, 195,715; unimproved, 180,823. Cash value, 3,500,000.

Annual products: corn, 515,000 bushels; wheat, 2,000 bushels; oats, 160,000 bushels; rye, 2,500 bushels; pease, 9,000 bushels; Irish potatoes, 25,000 bushels; sweet potatoes, 5,200 bushels; rice, 2,000 bushels; cotton, 60,000 pounds; wool, 22,000 pounds; butter, 150,000 pounds; cheese, 5,000 pounds; flax, 5,000 pounds; honey, 39,000 pounds: beeswax, 5,000 pounds; hay, 8,000 tons; molasses, sorghum, 9,000 gallons; fruits, value, $2,500; vegetables, value, $10,000.

Stock: horses, 3,950; mules, 500; cattle, 13,228; sheep, 14,000; hogs, 50,000.

Native Forests: ash, poplar, elm, hickory, oak, chestnut.

The lands are adapted to wheat, tobacco and fruits. Health good. A number of copper mines in the county.

Greensboro', the county seat, is 80 miles west of Raleigh. Female college at this place.

The North Carolina Central Rail Road, runs through this county. A Rail Road connects Greensboro' with Danville, Va. It will soon be connected by Rail Road with Salem also. High Point, on the N. C. Rail Road, is a good location for a village.

HALIFAX.

This county was organized from Edgecombe, in 1858.

Area, 680 square miles.

Population, 19,441.

Surface broken. Soil rich.

Farms, 900: acres improved, 147,615; unimproved, 248,825. Cash value, $3,699,426.

Annual products: corn, 800,000 bushels; wheat, 36,000 bushels; oats, 54,000 bushels; rye, 1,000 bushels; pease, 45,000 bushels; Irish potatoes, 16,000 bushels; sweet potatoes, 123,000 bushels; butter, 50,000 pounds; cotton, 4,200,000 pounds; wool, 9,000 pounds; tobacco, 900,000 pounds; honey, 15,000 pounds; beeswax, 2,000 pounds; hay, 6,500 tons; wine, 3,000 gallons; fruits, value $16,500.

Stock: horses, 1,994; mules, 1,500; cattle, 11,500; sheep, 5,000; hogs, 36,500.

Native growth: cedar, juniper, oak, hickory, ash and elm.

Churches, 20; doctors, 30; lawyers, 8; academies, 6; post offices, 8; mills, 10.

The rich valley of the Roanoke bounds the county on north and east. The lands are immensely rich. The high lands and recovered swamp lands are very productive of corn, cotton and fruits. Many of these lands lie on the rail roads leading to Norfolk and Petersburg and are favorably located for truck-farming.

HALIFAX, the county seat on the Roanoke river, is 87 miles north east from Raleigh. The Wilmington and Weldon and the Raleigh and Gaston Rail Roads run through this county.

HARNETT.

This county lies in the centre of the State.

Area, —— square miles.

Population, 8,000.

Farms, ——; acres improved, 216,670; unimproved, 241,-000. Cash value, $992,500.

Annual products: corn, 191,250 bushels; wheat 13,000 bushels; oats, 8,260 bushels; rye, 2,000 bushels; Irish potatoes, 4,000; sweet potatoes, 110,000 bushels; pease, 2,700; butter, 28,000 pounds; wool, 7,000 pounds; honey, 2,500 gallons.

Stock: cattle, 7,500; sheep, 5,000; hogs, 17,000.

Native growth: long leaf pine, oak, elm, &c.

Churches, 15. Mills, grist, 22. Postoffices, 7. Doctors, 12. Lawyers, 8.

The lands are adapted to cotton, corn and grape growing. The pine timber of the county is valuable.

LILLINGTON, the county seat, is 35 miles from Raleigh.

HAYWOOD.

This county was formed from Buncombe county in 1808. It lies in the mountain region.

Area, 900 square miles.

Population, 7,525.

It is drained by Pigeon river and its tributaries.

Farms, 650; acres improved, 35,000; acres unimproved, 350,000.

Annual products: corn, 200,000 bushels; wheat, 15,000 bushels; oats, 50,000 bushels; Irish and sweet potatoes, 15,000 bushels; butter, 60,000 pounds; hay, 10,000 tons.

Stock: horses and mules, 2,000; cattle, 8,000; sheep, 8,250; hogs, 18,500.

Natural forest: mountain ash, sugar maple, hickory, oak, chestnut, &c.

Churches, 26; 4 academies and a few primary schools.

The climate is lovely beyond description, and its mountain scenery is beautiful. Grain, fruits and the grasses, can be cultivated to a very great extent and its mountain ranges are favorable for raising large quantities of sheep, horses, &c.

Lands are abundant, fertile and cheap.

WAYNESVILLE the county seat, is situated in the forks of Pigeon river amid beautiful mountain scenery. Distance from Raleigh about 295 miles.

HENDERSON.

This county was formed out of Buncombe in 1858.

Area, 600 square miles.

Population, 10,500.

Farms, 500: acres improved, 43,500; unimproved, 150,500. Cash value, $1,515,000.

Annual products: corn, 326,000 bushels; wheat, 7,000 bushels; oats, 16,000 bushels; rye, 32,500 bushels; Irish potatoes, 18,000 bushels; sweet potatoes, 15,000 bushels; pease, 1,500 bushels; butter, 50,000 pounds; honey, 12,000 pounds; wool, 14,000 pounds; tobacco, 2,000 pounds; sorghum, 10,000 gallons; hay, 1,000 tons; fruits, value, $16,000.

Stock: horses, 1,400; mules, 450; cattle, 6,500; sheep, 8,000; hogs, 15,750.

Churches, 22; schools, 6; mills, grist, 12; doctors, 6; lawyers, 4.

The surface is broken. Lands good and well adapted to grazing. The bottom lands are very good.

HENDERSONVILLE, the county seat, is 250 miles west by South from Raleigh.

The Western Rail Road is to run through this county.

HERTFORD.

This county, named after the Earl of Hertford, was formed out of Chowan, Bertie and Northampton counties in 1759.

Area, 320 square miles.

Population, 10,000.

Surface, level. Soil very productive.

Farms, 500; acres improved, 72,550; unimproved, 133,500; cash value, $1,321,500.

Annual products: corn, 407,500 bushels; wheat, 10,600 bushels; oats, 11,750 bushels; rye, 1,000 bushels; Irish potatoes, 10,000 bushels; sweet potatoes, 120,000, bushels; pease,

28,000 bushels; cotton, 1,000,000 pounds; wool, 5,705 pounds; butter, 12.000 pounds; honey, 7,000 pounds; wine, 2,500 gallons; fish, 2,000 barrels; hay, 2,500 tons; fruits, value, $10,000.

Stock: horses, 1,144; mules, 500; cattle, 4,400; sheep, 3,500; hogs, 21,500.

Trees, natural: pine, oak, juniper, elm and cedar.

Churches, 20; colleges, 2, academies, 8; post offices, 6; mills, grist, 12; saw, 4; doctors, 14; lawyers, 4.

The lands of this county are good—well adapted to cotton and corn. Several fine fisheries in this county lie on Chowan river. Pine and cypress timber valuable.

WINTON, on the Chowan river, is the county seat.

Murfreesboro' on the Meherrin river, is the principal town. It has two Female Colleges, and is a pleasant place.

HYDE.

This county, named after General Hyde, was one of the original precincts of 1729.

Area, 430 square miles.

Population, 8,000.

Surface level. Soil rich.

Farms, 300; acres improved, 32,000; unimproved, 90,500. Cash value, $1,700,000.

Annual product: corn, 500,000 bushels; wheat, 25,000 bushels; oats, 2,500 bushels; rye, 1,200 bushels; Irish potatoes, 100; sweet potatoes, 8,100; pease, 3,500 bushels; cotton, 200,000 pounds; wool, 510,000 pounds; honey, 1,500 pounds.

Stock: horses, 900; mules, 150; cattle, 6,600; hogs, 11,500.

Trees, natural: red cedar, oak, cypress, gum, long leaf pine, juniper and hickory.

Mills: grist, 3; saw, 4; shingle, 4. Ministers, 7; doctors, 7; lawyers, 2.

Lands very rich, especially around Mattamuskeet Lake. It is one of the finest corn sections in the world. Peat is abundant in the county. Juniper and cypress timber very valuable.

SWAN QUARTER, the county seat, near Pamlico, is 170 miles east from Raleigh.

IREDELL.

This county, named after Judge Iredell, was formed from Rowan county in 1788.

Area, 600 square miles.

Population, 15,500.

Surface hilly, soil, generally productive.

Farms 1,200: acres improved, 96,000; unimproved, 227,000. Cash value, $2,500,000.

Annual products: corn, 505,000 bushels; wheat, 135,000 bushels; oats, 72,000 bushels; rye, 1,500 bushels; Irish potatoes, 10,500 bushels; sweet potatoes, 25,000 bushels; pease, 12,500 bushels; cotton, 200,000 pounds; wool, 15,000 pounds; tobacco, 150,000 pounds; butter, 84,000 pounds; honey, 56,500 pounds; beeswax, 4,000 pounds; flax, 250,000 pounds; sorghum, 8,500 gallons; hay, 4,000 tons; fruits, value, $14,000.

Stock: horses, 5,000; mules, 1,000; cattle, 11,000; hogs, 26,000.

Trees, natural: ash, chestnut, oak and hickory.

Churches, 40; colleges, 2; academies, 4; other schools; mills, grist, 15; oil,—; tanneries, 10; factories, cotton, 1; tobacco, 4; post offices, 15; ministers, 15; doctors, 25; lawyers, 8.

This is a good wheat, corn and fruit county. Tobacco also grows well, and cotton on its southern border.

STATESVILLE, the county seat, is 145 miles west from Raleigh. A female college here.

The Western and Charlotte Rail Roads run through this county.

JACKSON.

This county was organized out of Haywood and Macon counties in 1850, and lies in the south western part of the State. Formerly inhabited by the Cherokee Indians of whom a few hundred still remain.

Area, 1,308 square miles.

Population 5,500.

Farms 500; 46,772 acres improved; 775,000 acres unimproved. Much of this is said not to be enlisted and is the property of the State. Perhaps 500,000 acres are in market.

Of the small portion cultivated, the annual product was in 1860, wheat, 18,000 bushels; corn 237,997 bushels; oats 11,000 bushels; beans and peas, 3.000 bushels; Irish potatoes 16,000 bushels; sweet potatoes 15,500; tobacco, 7,000 pounds; wool. 9,000 pounds; butter, 42,000 pounds; honey, 16,000 pounds; molasses, 10,000 gallons; hay, 500 tons; orchard products valued at $5,000.

Stock: horses, 1660; mules, 204; milch cows, 1916; other cattle, 4223; sheep, 5336; hogs, 16,168.

Original growth of timber: oak, hickory, chesnut, poplar. locust and walnut. Immense forests still remain untouched.

Lands vary from poor to very good. Valleys and mountain sides fertile and very productive. A fine grazing country. Lands from $1 to $5 per acre.

Mines of gold, copper, &c., abundant. Limestone all over this region.

Churches, 10; lawyers, 2; doctors 4; grist mills, 6; post offices 8.

WEBSTER is the county seat of Jackson.

JOHNSTON.

This county was formed out of Craven, 1746, and named after Gov. Johnston.

Area, 670 square miles.

Population, 15,600.

Farms, 1,200; 110,000 acres improved; 225,000 acres unimproved.

Stock: horses, 2,225; mules, 600; cows, 4,550; other cattle, 6,500; sheep, 8,500; hogs, 40,500.

Annual products: wheat, 6,000 bushels; rye, 10,000 bushels; corn, 468,500 bushels; oats, 22,800, bushels; rice, 2,500 pounds; tobacco, 15,000 pounds; cotton, 3,000 bales; wool, 11,000 pounds; pease, 80,000 bushels; Irish potatoes, 5,000 bushels; sweet potatoes, 225,000 bushels; orchard products, $10,000; butter, 70,000 pounds; hay, 4,000 tons; honey, 15,000 pounds.

Churches, 23; academies 6; lawyers, 9; doctors 12; factory, cotton, 1; post offices, 6.

Granite and iron are found at different places. It is well watered by Neuse and Little rivers, and a number of creeks.

Original growth of timber: pine, oak, hickory, gum, elm, ash and black jack.

A portion of the lands are sandy, but generally good and productive. Good cotton farms found in all parts of the county.

The North Carolina Rail Road runs through the county.

Land, in any quantity for sale very low.

SMITHFIELD is the county seat. It lies on Neuse river 26 miles from Raleigh and about the same distance West from Goldsboro.

JONES.

This county was formed in 1779, from Craven, and lies in the Eastern part of the State.

Area, 380 square miles.

Population 5,750.

Farms, 300; acres improved, 55,000; acres unimproved, 125,000. Cash value, $1,000,000.

Stock: horses, 825; mules, 350; cows, 1,500; other cattle, 3,000; sheep, 3,500; hogs, 1,600.

Annual products: wheat, 1,500 bushels; oats, 2,600 bushels; corn, 250,000 bushels; cotton, 2,000 bales; wool, 7,000 pounds; pease, 25,000 bushels; Irish potatoes, 4,000 bushels; sweet potatoes, 100,000 bushels; lumber, tar and turpentine exported.

Churches, 15; academies, 6; lawyers, 1; doctors, 5; grist and saw mills, 12; steam mills, 2; post offices, 4.

It is watered by Trent river and a number of creeks. Trent river is navigable to Pollocksville.

Native trees: cedar, juniper, cypress, oak and gum.

Marl and muck in abundance. Lands cheap, and produce corn and cotton finely.

TRENTON is the county seat, 125 miles Southeast from Raleigh and about 20 miles fıom New Bern.

LENOIR.

This county was formed in 1791, out of Johnston and lies in the eastern part of the State.

Area, 450 square miles.

Population, 10,223.

Farms, 500; acres improved, 112,000; acres unimproved, 162,000.

Stock: horses, 1,230; mules, 700; cows, 1,500; other cattle, 4,500; sheep, 3,500; hogs, 25,000.

Annual products: wheat, 12,000 bushels; rye 2,500 bushel; corn, 240,000 bushels; oats, 2,000 bushels; rice, 15,000 pounds; cotton, 4,500 bales; wool, 6,000 pounds; peas 8,500 bushels; Irish potatoes, 7,000 bushels; sweet potatoes, 90,000 bushels; butter 16,750 pounds; honey, 10,000 pounds.

Churches, 15; academies, 6; lawyers, 6; doctors, 12; grist mills, 12; saw mills, 6; post offices, 5.

The Atlantic Rail Road runs through this county. Steamboats ply between Kinston and New Berne.

This is a splendid county for cotton, corn and truck farming. Soil good and very productive.

A large quantity of valuable land is in the market at low prices.

Natural forest: oak, pine, gum, ash and cypress.

KINSTON the county seat lies on Neuse River, 80 miles south east from Raleigh. Steamboats from New Berne, come here and the Atlantic Rail Road runs through this place.

LINCOLN.

This county was formerly called Tyron, after Gov. Tyron, but whose oppressive administration was so obnoxious, that the General Assembly changed it to Lincoln in 1779. It lies in the south western part of the State.

Area, 420 square miles.

Population 10,100.

Farms, 800; acres improved, 45,567; acres unimproved, 140,000; cash value $1,380,500.

Stock: horses and mules, 2,100; cows, 1,800; other cattle, 3,000; sheep, 5,100; hogs, 13,000.

Annual products: wheat, 65,000 bushels; rye, 500 bushels; corn, 270,000 bushels; oats, 16,500 bushels; tobacco, 7,000 pounds; cotton, 500 bales; wool, 8,000 pounds; pease, 7,000 bushels; Irish potatoes, 6,000 bushels; sweet potatoes, 23,000 bushels; orchard products $11,000; butter, 75,000 pounds; hay, 3,000 tons; sorghum, 10,000 gallons; honey, 26,000 pounds.

There are 3 cotton factories; 7 iron foundries; 2 iron forges; 30 grist mills; 2 paper mills; 10 saw mills; 10 tanneries; churches, 32; academies, 10; lawyers, 13; doctors, 15; ministers, 20; gold mines, 10; post offices 9.

Catawba river runs through the county. It is rich in mineral ores and is also a good farming county.

Forest: ash, elm, white and red oak, chestnut, poplar, &c.

LINCOLN is the county seat, 170 miles south west, from Raleigh. The Rutherfordton Rail Road runs through this county and village.

MACON.

This county was formed in 1828, from Haywood, and lies in the extreme west.

Area, 600 square miles.

Farms, 700: 32,600 acres improved; 305,000 acres unimproved. Cash value, $900,000.

Stock: horses, 1,500; mules, 600; cows, 1,800; other cattle, 5,000, sheep, 5,100; hogs, 26,700.

Annual products: wheat, 65,000 bushels; rye, 1,000 bushels; corn, 270,000 bushels; oats, 16,500 bushels; tobacco, 20,000 pounds; wool, 8,000 pounds; pease, 10,000 bushels; Irish potatoes, 6,000 bushels; sweet potatoes, 25,000 bushels; orchard products, 12,000; butter, 75,000 pounds; hay, 3,000 tons; sorghum, 10,000 gallons; honey, 26,000 pounds; home manufactures, $18,500.

Churches, 30; academies, 4; lawyers, 4; doctors, 5; ministers, 18; post offices, 4.

The surface is broken and mountainous. Soil, ordinary to good. Fine grazing region.

The Western Rail Road will run through this county.

Forests: oak, sugar maple, locust and white and black pine.

The beautiful red marble mountain is here.

In this county, thousands of sheep, cattle, horses and mules could be raised at a small cost. Three hundred thousand acres of mountain and farming lands in the market from 70 cents to five dollars per acre. Copper ore all over the county.

It is capable of supporting a population of fifty thousand.

FRANKLIN is the county seat, 325 miles from Raleigh.

MADISON.

This county was formed in 1850, from Buncombe and Yancey, named after President Madison.

Area, 450 square miles.

Population, 6,000.

Acres improved, 32,500; acres unimproved 174,000. Cash value, $750,000.

Stock: horses, 1,200; mules, 200; sheep, 5,100; cows, 2,100; other cattle, 3,000; hogs, 15,000.

Annual products: wheat, 32,500 bushels; rye, 3,000 bushels; corn, 235,500 bushels; oats, 30,000 bushels; tobacco, 16,000 pounds; wool, 10,000 pounds; pease, 5,000 bushels; Irish potatoes, 15,000 bushels; sweet potatoes, 3,000 bushels; orchard products, $12,000; butter, 58,000 pounds; flax, 5,000 pounds; sorghum, 25,000 gallons; honey, 20,000 pounds; home manufactures, $30,000.

Churches, 12; lawyers, 2; doctors, 4; ministers, 6; post offices, 6; mills, 10.

Original forests: pine, ash, elm, balsam, chestnut.

This is a beautiful county. Surface rough and mountainous. Lands good. A splendid farming, fruit and grazing region. Lands cheap and abundant. It is spoken of as one of the finest counties in the future in the transmontane region, when Rail Roads penetrate it.

MARSHALL is the county seat, about 260 miles west from Raleigh, on the east side of the French Broad.

MARTIN.

This county was organized in 1794, from Halifax, and named after Gov. Martin, the last of the Colonial Governors.

It lies on the Roanoke river.
Area, 450 square miles.
Population 10,119.
Farms, 600; acres improved, 56,000; acres unimproved, 178,500; cash value, $1,158,545
Stock: horses, 1,156; mules, 551; cows, 1,828; other cattle, 5,000; sheep, 4,780; hogs, 21,241.
Annual products: wheat, 2,500 bushels; corn, 320,000 bushels; oats, 17,000 bushels; rice, 2,500 pounds; cotton, 3,500 bales; wool, 8,000 pounds; pease, 35,000 bushels; Irish potatoes, 7,000 bushels; sweet potatoes, 100,000 bushels; orchard productions, $1,000; wine, 5,000 gallons; butter, 12,000 pounds; beeswax, 2,500 pounds; honey, 1,700 pounds.
Churches, 15; academies, 5; lawyers, 8; doctors, 7; merchants, 20; grist mills, 8; saw mills, 6; post offices, 4.
Original growth of timber: pine, oak, hickory, cypress and juniper.
This county is partly sandy. Soil good, low grounds very rich. The swamps are filled with vast quantities of juniper and cypress, fit for lumber. The Tarboro and Williamston Rail Road will pass through this county. There are rich beds of marl of the best kind for improving lands.
Cotton, corn, and the grape are cultivated largely.
WILLIAMSTON is the county seat, on the Roanoke river, 140 miles East from Raleigh. A handsome town.

McDOWELL.

This county was formed in 1842 from Rutherford and Burke.
Area, 450 square miles.
Population, 7,100.
Farms, 600; acres improved, 28,878; acres unimproved, 115,500. Cash value, $775,000.
Stock: horses, 900; mules, 600; cows, 1,500; other cattle, 3,000; sheep, 3,700; hogs 12,000.
Annual products: wheat, 25,000 bushels; rye, 5,500 bushels; corn, 240,000 bushels; oats, 6,000 bushels; tobacco, 20,000 pounds; wool, 8,000 pounds; pease, 7,000 bushels; Irish potatoes, 9,000 bushels; sweet potatoes, 14,000; butter, 30,000 pounds; sorghum, 3,000 gallons; honey, 11,000 pounds.
Churches, 20; lawyers, 3; doctors, 9; academies, 4; gold mines, 4; grist mills 10; post offices, 6.
The Western Rail Road passes through this county.
Original forests: white pine, ash, oak, chestnut, laurel, balsam, &c.

Catawba and Linville rivers, and a number of creeks water the county.

Surface broken and mountainous. Much good farming land. A fine fruit and grazing region.

MARION is the county seat, 200 miles from Raleigh.

MECKLENBURG.

This county was formed in 1762 from Anson, and named in honor of Queen Charlotte of Mecklenburg.

Area, 720 square miles.

Population, 17,500.

Acres improved, 95,938; unimproved, 181,562; cash value, $2,823,949.

Stock: horses, 2,829; mules, 1,500; cows, 4,319; other cattle 6,500; sheep, 9,216; hogs, 23,500.

Annual products: wheat, 160,000 bushels; rye, 1,299; corn, 550,225 bushels; oats, 43,366 bushels; tobacco, 25,161 bushels; cotton, 6,112 bales; wool, 15,621 pounds; pease, 41,596 bushels; Irish potatoes, 11,835 bushels; sweet potatoes, 26,716 bushels; orchard products $5,000; butter, 129,269; hay, 2,553 tons; sorghum, 13,283 gallons; beeswax, 1,429 pounds; honey, 20,384 pounds.

Churches, 35; ministers, 23; colleges, 3; academies 6; schools, primary 40; lawyers, 11; doctors, 25; 1 woolen factory; factories of different kinds about 20; mines: gold and copper, 15; grist mills, 25; post offices, 10.

Gold is found all over the county.

Natural forest: ash, elm, oaks, pine, chestnut, &c.

It is thought by scientific men that the mines in North Carolina, are as valuable, as the mines in California.

The soil produces wheat, corn, apples, pears, peaches, hay, clover and garden vegetables in great profusion.

The lands are well adapted to cotton and corn.

CHARLOTTE is the county seat of justice for Mecklenburg county, it lies 155 miles southwest from Raleigh. It is a city of growing improvement. It was here, the first Declaration of American Independence was read, on the 20th of May, 1775.

MITCHELL.

This county has recently been formed out of Yancey, McDowell, Burke and Watauga, and named after the late Rev. Dr. Mitchell of Chapel Hill.

Being a new county, its statistics have not been ascertained.

Its lands are good. Surface broken and mountainous.

Wheat, corn, rye, oats, Irish potatoes, buckwheat, cabbages and fruits, especially apples, grow well. It is particularly adapted to stock raising and grazing.

Much of it is in original forests, of ash, poplar, chestnut, white pine, balsam, oak, &c.

Iron and copper ores have been found and are believed to exist in large quantities.

In the Northeastern part of the county, limestone, blue and white marble of fine texture are said to exist.

The lands are very cheap and abundant. The resources of the county are yet to be developed.

BAKERSVILLE is the county seat.

MONTGOMERY.

This county was taken from Anson in 1779.

Area, 550 square miles.

Population, 7,640.

Acres improved, 56,178 acres; unimproved, 204,513. Cash value, $359,500.

Annual products: wheat, 66,772 bushels; rye, 1,000 bushels; corn, 281,658 bushels; oats, 35,246 bushels; tobacco, 25,000 pounds; cotton, 1,500 bales; pease, 11,000; Irish potatoes, 8,000 bushels; sweet potatoes, 35,000 bushels; orchard production $7,500; butter 80,000 pounds; hay, 1,729 tons; sorghum, 3,000 gallons; honey, 25,000 pounds.

Stock: horses, 1,354; mules, 250; cows, 2,259; other cattle, 5,000; sheep, 7,500; hogs, 14,000.

Churches, 20; ministers, 15; doctors, 6; lawyers, 4; academies 6, besides primary schools; grist mills, 28; saw mills, 4; cotton factories, 2; several tanneries; gold mines, 9, others opening; post offices, 10.

Forests: white oak, red oak, post oak, hickory, persimmon, ash, poplar, &c.

The minerals of this county are very valuable.

Its water power is very great, suitable for machinery of all kinds.

Lands adapted to cotton, corn, potatoes, &c. Can be bought low.

TROY is the county seat, about 90 miles Southwest from Raleigh.

MOORE.

This county was organized in 1784, from Cumberland.

Area, 650 square miles.

Population 11,475.

Acres improved, 65,165; acres unimproved, 345,148; cash value, $1,178,311.

Stock: horses, 2,160; mules, 300; cows, 3,589; other cattle, 6,500; sheep, 12,866; hogs, 25,000.

Annual products: wheat, 75,000 bushels; rye, 5,000 bushels; corn, 281,650 bushels; oats, 35,500 bushels; wool, 17,500 pounds; pease, 25,000 bushels; Irish potatoes, 2,500 bushels; sweet potatoes, 77,000 bushels: orchard products, $10,000; butter, 115,000 pounds; hay, 500 tons; turpentine, &c.

Churches, 30; ministers, 18; doctors, 12; lawyers, 2, academies, 6, and primary schools in the county; grist mills, 20.

Mines: two gold mines and one soap stone mine have been worked; post offices, 7.

Original growth of timber: long leaf pine, red oak, black jack, hickory, poplar, &c.

The lands range from poor to good. Cotton, corn, sweet potatoes and pease grow well, and the grape may be raised extensively. It is well timbered with long leaf pine, but is rather inaccessible to market. Land can be bought very low.

The Fayetteville, (Coalfields) Rail Road passes through the Northern part of this county.

CARTHAGE, the county seat, is 60 miles from Raleigh.

NASH.

This county was formed out of Edgecombe in 1777, and named after General Francis Nash, who fell at the battle of Germanton.

Area, 600 square miles.

Population, 11,688.

Acres improved, 81,100; acres unimproved, 205,000. Cash value, $1,736,608.

Stock: horses, 1,116; mules, 500; cows, 2,199; other cattle, 3,536; oxen, 1,145; sheep, 5,439; hogs, 25,874.

Annual products: wheat, 12,000 bushels; rye, 1,000 bushels; corn, 335,000 bushels; oats, 20,500 bushels; tobacco, 100,000 pounds; cotton, 3,000 bales; wool, 7,000 pounds; pease, 30,000 bushels; Irish potatoes, 8,000 bushels; sweet potatoes, 115,800 bushels; orchard products, $15,000; butter, 23,885 pounds; beeswax, 1,500 pounds; honey, 15,671 pounds.

Churches, 22; schools, 6; mines, 1; post offices, 4.

Native forests: oak, ashe, pine, gum, &c.

Its soil is sandy, but productive. Cotton, corn, potatoes, &c., grow finely. Marl and muck are easily obtained. Fruits grow well. The county has been famous for apple and peach brandy. Lands are cheap.

NASHVILLE is the county seat, and about 44 miles from Raleigh.

NEW HANOVER.

This county was organized in 1728, named after the Royal House of Hanover.

Area, 1000 square miles.

Surface level. Soil sandy, but productive.

Population 25,000.

Farms, 650; acres, improved, 52,925; acres, unimproved, 395,624; cash value, $1,381,687.

Stock: horses 1,151; mules, 439; cows, 3,435; other cattle, 9,000; sheep, 5,758; hogs, 30,000.

Annual products: wheat, 9,630 bushels; rye, 1,500 bushels; corn, 250,000 bushels; oats, 1,000 bushels; rice, 1,500,000 pounds; wool, 7,000 pounds; pease, 82,000 bushels; Irish potatoes, 5,500 bushels; sweet potatoes, 175,000 bushels; pea nuts, 100,000 bushels; lumber, $50,000; turpentine, 10,000 barrels; spirits of turpentine, 20,000 barrels; tar, fish, &c.

Mills, Factories, &c.: 6 saw mills; 4 planing mills; 15 turpentine distilleries; 30 tar factories; 2 ship yards.

Churches, 20; ministers, 12; academies, 8; lawyers, 10; doctors, 15; grist mills, 8.

Forests: principally long leaf pine, some oak, hickory and live oak.

The lands are well adapted to truck farming. The pea-nut is more extensively cultivated than in any county in the State and is very profitable. Cotton and corn do well, and the rice lands are productive.

WILMINGTON the largest city of the State, is also the county seat of New Hanover. It is constantly growing in commercial importance. Large exports of cotton, turpentine and lumber are annually made from this city.

NORTHAMPTON.

This county was formed in 1741, and was taken from Bertie.

Area, 350 square miles.

Population, 13,500.

127,775 acres improved; 170,292 acres unimproved. Cash value, $2,639,030.

Stock: horses, 1,882; mules 1,950; cows, 2,933; other cattle, 6,000; sheep, 3,000; hogs, 32,800.

Annual products: wheat, 30,000 bushels; rye, 1,000 bushels; corn, 635,000 bushels; oats, 25,000 bushels; tobacco, 300,000 pounds; cotton, 6,500 bales; wool, 7,500 pounds; pease 54,500 bushels; Irish potatoes, 10,000 bushels; sweet potatoes, 110,000 bushels; orchard products $5,000; butter 110,000 pounds; honey, 6,000 pounds.

Churches, 10; schools, 10; lawyers, 5; doctors 12; hotels, 2; mills, 6; post offices, 6; 6 stave factories; 1 shingle mill.

Original growth of timber: ash, oak, cypress, pine, &c.

The surface is level, the soil productive, and accessible to market.

It is well adapted to corn, cotton, truck farming and the cultivation of the grape.

JACKSON is the county seat, and located in the midst of a rich farming country.

ONSLOW.

This county was organized 1754, from New Hanover. It lies in the eastern part of the State.

Area, 600 square miles.

Population, 8,856.

Acres improved, 65,000; acres unimproved, 250,000. Cash value, $1,337,923.

Annual products: wheat, 500 bushels; rye, 5,000 bushels; corn, 275,000 bushels; oats, 3,000 bushels; rice, 50,000 pounds; wool, 7,500 pounds; pease, 85,500 bushels; Irish potatoes, 6,500 bushels; sweet potatoes, 175,500 bushels; butter, 20,000 pounds; beeswax, 5,000 pounds; honey, 50,000 pounds; cotton, 500,000 pounds; turpentine, $10,000; Lumber, $5,000.

Stock: horses, 1,000; mules, 500; cows, 2,619; other cattle, 6,500; sheep, 4,000; hogs, 25,600

Churches, 22; academies, 5; lawyers, 2; doctors, 12; post offices, 7.

Forests: long leaf pine, oak, gum and cypress.

Lands productive and well adapted to cotton and corn, and the cultivation of the grape. Pine and cypress lumber valuable.

JACKSONVILLE is the county seat, 120 miles South-east from Raleigh.

ORANGE.

This county was organized in 1751, from Granville, Johnston and Bladen, and named in compliment to the Roya House of England. It lies in the centre of the State.

Area, 650 square miles.

Population, 16,429.

Farms, 1,230; acres, improved, 101,354; acres unimproved, 246,040; cash value, $2,141,690.

Stock: horses, 3,199; mules, 350; cows, 4,081; other cattle, 5,999; sheep, 11,314; hogs, 27,444.

Annual products: wheat, 154,794 bushels; rye, 2,527 bushels;

corn, 400,242 bushels; oats, 81,825 bushels; tobacco, 1,139,-764 pounds; wool, 15,004 pounds; pease, 8,506 bushels; Irish potatoes, 12,754 bushels; sweet potatoes, 46,716 bushels; orchard products, $5,000; butter, 105,884 pounds; hay, 1,500 tons; flax, 5,000 pounds; bees wax, 2,500 pounds; honey, 20,000 pounds.

Original growth of timber: white oak, red oak, post oak, cedar, hickory, walnut, elm, oak, poplar, tulip tree, gum, persimmon, black jack, &c.

The soil is principally of red clay, adapted to wheat, corn, tobacco, oats and fruits. It is well watered, healthy, and a good farming country.

HILLSBORO, the county seat, was laid out in 1759.

It has a large Female school of high reputation, and two Academies.

At Chapel Hill, the State Uuiversity is located.

Durham, on the North Carolina Rail Road is a thriving village.

PASQUOTANK.

This county was known in 1729, as one of the original precints of ancient Albemarle. It derives its name from an Indian tribe. It lies in the Northeastern part of the State.

Area, 250 square miles.

Population, 8,940.

Farms 600; acres improved, 53,662; unimproved, 40,200; cash value $2,000,000.

Stock: horses, 1,100; mules, 554; cows, 1,500; other cattle, 4,000; sheep, 1,515; hogs, 15,500.

Annual products: wheat, 75,000 bushels; rye, 40,000 bushels; corn, 600,000 bushels; oats, 6,000 bushels; wool, 7,000 pounds: peas, 12,700 bushels; Irish potatoes, 3,750 bushels; sweet potatoes, 35,000 bushels; butter 22,500 pounds; flax, 10,000 pounds; honey, 10,000 pounds.

Churches, 17; schools, 12; teachers, 23; 3 steam mills that manufacture flour, corn, lumber, &c.; 2 post offices.

Original growth: gum, ash, cypress, &c.

The soil mostly a deep and very rich alluvial soil. Very productive and almost inexhaustible. Corn, wheat and flax are produced in great quantities, without manure. Lands high, though lower than formerly.

The lands in some parts of the county have been cultivated in corn for one hundred years in succession, and without manure, yet they produce now from 30 to 40 bushels of corn per acre, with ordinary culture.

ELIZABETH CITY is the county seat, 215 miles from Raleigh.

PERQUIMANS.

This county was the earliest permanent settlement in the State. Its name comes from an Indian tribe who were found here when the English landed.

It lies in the North-eastern part of the State.

The first settlement, was made in 1662, after the expulsion of the Quakers from Virginia., who came over into North Carolina and settled here. The oldest land title in North Carolina is the grant of King Yeopim, an Indian Chief, to George Durant, who settled Durant's Neck, a promontory on Albemarle Sound.

Area, 250 square miles.

Population 7,248.

Farms, 550; acres improved, 52,182; acres unimproved, 67,-852; cash value, $1,537,970.

Stock: horses, 1,791; mules, 650; cows, 1,635; other cattle, 4,500; sheep, 2,743; hogs, 16,413.

Annual products: wheat, 99,834 bushels; rye, 1,000 bushels; corn, 605,000 bushels; oats, 4,500; wool, 9,500 pounds; pease, 13,500 bushels; Irish potatoes, 6,100 bushels; sweet potatoes, 75,000 bushels; orchard products, $2,500; butter, 25,000 pounds; hay, 2,000 tons; flax, 6,500 pounds; beeswax, 1,225 pounds; honey, 20,000 pounds.

Churches 15; lawyers, 5; doctors, 9; grist mills, 4; steam mills, 5; post offices, 6.

Original forests: oak, gum, cypress, &c. Lumber valuable.

The lands are of the first quality for wheat, clover, corn and grapes. Large fisheries of shad, rock and herring are located on the sound and rivers.

HERTFORD is the county seat, situated on Perquimans river, 194 miles from Raleigh.

PERSON.

This county was formed in 1791, out of Caswell, and is located in the northern part of the State.

Area. 370 square miles.

Population, 11,500.

Farms, 700: acres improved, 101,756; acres unimproved, 118,662. Cash value, $2,000,000.

Stock: horses, 2,034; mules, 300; cows, 2,500; other cattle, 4,000; sheep, 8,155; hogs, 16,500.

Annual products: wheat, 85,000 bushels; rye, 1,000 bushels; corn, 265,500 bushels; oats, 110,000 bushels; tobacco, 3,000,000 pounds; cotton, 500 bales; wool, 10,000 pounds; pease, 4,000 bushels; Irish potatoes, 6,500 bushels; sweet potatoes, 35,000 bushels; orchard products, $2,500; butter, 75,000 pounds; flax, 2.000 pounds; beeswax, 2.000 pounds; honey, 20,000 pounds; home manufactures, $1.850.

Churches, 30; academies, 4; other schools, 6; ministers, lawyers and doctors, grist mills numerous; post offices, 8; tobacco factories, 4; tanneries, 6.

Natural growth: oak, poplar, ash, hickory, gum, elm, &c.

Surface, rolling; soil, of good quality, especially on Hyco River, for tobacco, wheat, corn and fruits, especially apples, peaches, pears, &c.

Its climate is healthy and water pure. Some farms well improved.

ROXBOROUGH is the county seat, and lies in a high healthy location.

PITT.

This county was organized out of Beaufort in 1760. Called after Sir William Pitt of England.

Surface level. Soil sandy and rich loam. Large quantities of marl are found in nearly every part of the county.

Area, 650 square miles.

Population, 16,000.

Farms, 830; 101,164 acres improved; 250,000 acres unimproved.

Natural growth of timber: red and post oak, long leaf pine, &c.

Stock: horses 2,000; mules, 1,100; cows 3,500; other cattle, 8,000; sheep, 5,000; hogs, 38,600.

Annual products: wheat, 12,700 bushels; rye, 6,000 bushels; corn, 710,000 bushels; oats, 17,250 bushels; rice, 55,000 pounds; cotton, 7,500 bales; wool, 7,374 pounds; pease, 74,000 bushels; Irish potatoes, 11,750 bushels; sweet potatoes, 186,000 bushels; orchard products, $6,500; wine, 2,500 gallons; butter, 35,000 pounds; hay, 4,617 tons; honey, 4,000 pounds.

Churches, 25; academies 6; and several primary schools in the county; 10 lawyers; 12 doctors; 15 ministers; 12 grist mills; 4 saw mills.

Its exports are lumber, tar, turpentine, crude and distilled, corn and cotton.

Steamboats ply between Greenville and Washington.

The soil in this county is generally rich and productive. There are also fine forests of pine for lumber. Soil suitable for growth of grapes, corn, cotton and pease.

GREENVILLE is the county seat, it lies on Tar river 100 miles east from Raleigh.

POLK.

This is one of the new counties organized out of Rutherford county in 1854, and named after James K. Polk, late President of the United States.

It lies in the Western part of the State, is well watered. Surface mountainous.

Area 300 square miles.

On the creeks and rivers are large bodies of good land easily cultivated, producing good crops of Indian corn, wheat, oats, rye, tobacco, sugar cane, buckwheat and some cotton.

No Rail Roads yet in operation.

The mountain ranges are equal to any for stock raising and growth of trees and fruit.

Mines: Pender's gold mine, it is said, some several hundred thousand dollars worth of gold have been taken.

Large quantities of gold lie on the borders of Pacolet and its tributaries. Double Branch, Red Spring, Prince and other mines, said to be rich, both in deposit and surface veins. South Fork and White Creek afford a splendid prospect for gold.

It is well timbered with oak, hickory, ash, &c., and rock of all kinds for building purposes.

There is a belt of land on the South side of Tryon and white oak mountains, that has several farms and orchards, where frost has never been known. Peaches of the finest kind and apples and grapes are cultivated.

Clover, grasses, hay, &c , can be grown abundantly. Lands sell from 75 cents to $3 per acre.

COLUMBUS is the county seat.

Population about 4,000.

Farms, 320; acres improved, 20,500; acres unimproved, 71,000.

Products: corn, 350,000 bushels; wheat, 25,000 bushels; oats, 19,000 bushels; rye, 2,500 bushels; cotton, 80,000 pounds; wool, 1,500 pounds; tobacco, 1,650 pounds; butter, 8,000 pounds.

Wild animals: racoon, opossum, squirrels, foxes, plenty of fish.

Fruit: unknown quantities.

Original growth of timber: white pine, sugar maple, walnut, oaks, &c.

RANDOLPH

This county was organized in 1779, from Guilford and Rowan. It lies in the centre of the State.

Area, 880 square miles.

Population, 16,500.

Farms, 1,112; acres improved, 191,486; unimproved, 288,-995.

The natural growth of the forest is white and red oak, hickory, elm and ash.

Stock: horses, 3,877; mules, 300; cows, 5,490; other cattle, 7,500; sheep, 18,137; hogs, 32,066.

Annual products: wheat, 227,654 bushels; rye, 1,663 bushels: corn, 400,000 bushels; oats, 60,000 bushels; rice, 5,000 pounds; tobacco, 85,000 pounds; wool, 27,000 pounds; pease, 8,000 bushels; Irish potatoes, 21,250 bushels; sweet potatoes, 50,000 bushels; orchard products, $31,118; butter, 140,000 pounds; cheese, 3,000 pounds; hay, 5,788 tons; flax, 5,000 pounds; maple molasses, 5,000 gallons; sorghum molasses, 2,000 gallons; beeswax, 6,000 pounds; honey, 75,000 pounds.

Churches, 40; academies, 12; ministers, 25; teachers, 15; lawyers, 6; doctors, 25; post offices, 18; grist mills, 26; 3 steam mills; 5 cotton factories; 1 woolen factory; 1 steam tannery; 1 foundry and extensive beds of slate underlies a large part of this county.

The soil is generally poor but productive in some sections. Land very cheap.

The lands are adapted to wheat, cotton, corn and fruits of all kinds. The Western (Fayetteville) Rail Road will probably pass through this county. Trinity college is located in the Northern part of this county.

Gold is found in different parts of the county. Several mines have been opened.

ASHBORO the county seat, is 72 miles West from Raleigh.

RICHMOND.

This county was formed in 1779, from Anson, named in honor of the Duke of Richmond. It lies in the southern part of the State.

Area, 900 square miles.

Population, 11,000.

Farms, 525; acres improved, 82,500; acres unimproved, 352,242.

Forest growth: oak, long leaf pine, ash, &c.

Stock: horses, 1,500; mules, 800; cows, 2,600; other cattle, 6,500; sheep, 4,500; hogs, 20,000.

Annual products: wheat, 32,500 bushels; rye, 3,000 bushels; corn, 265,000 bushels; oats, 25,000; rice, 5,000 pounds; cotton, 6,000 bales; wool, 8,500 pounds; pease 47,000 bushels; Irish potatoes, 7,000 bushels; sweet potatoes, 75,000 bushels; orchard products, $9,500; butter, 46,000 pounds; sorghum molasses, 2,000 gallons; honey, 10,000 pounds.

Churches, 20; schools, 4; academy and several primary schools; ministers, 15; teachers, 10; lawyers, 4; doctors, 6; grist mills, 5; cotton factories, 2; post offices, 10.

The Wilmington and Rutherford Rail Road runs through the county.

The Fayetteville and Albemarle Plank Road runs through the north part of the county.

Surface undulating. Soil good. Lands cheap. They produce cotton, corn and pease, abundantly. It is a fine grape growing region, as are all the eastern and south-eastern counties of the State.

ROCKINGHAM is the county seat, situated about the centre of the county.

ROBESON.

This county was organized in 1786 from Bladen, it lies in the Southern part of the State.

Area, 900 square miles.

Population, 15,500.

Farms, 1,250; acres improved, 106,150; acres unimproved, 464,904.

Natural forests: pine, oak, hickory, ash, gum, poplar, &c.

Surface level. Soil sandy and clay, interspersed with swamp lands rich. Cotton, corn, fruits and the grape grow finely. Lands are cheap.

Stock: horses, 2,275; mules, 900; cows, 4,000; other cattle, 8,696; sheep, 10,580; hogs, 40,000.

Annual products: wheat, 12,500 bushels; rye, 5,000 bushels; corn, 350,000 bushels; oats, 10,000 bushels; rice, 50,000 pounds; cotton, 3,500 bales; wool, 18,000 pounds; pease, 45,000 bushels; Irish potatoes, 5,000 bushels; sweet potatoes, 145,000 bushels; orchard products, $2,000; butter, 36,500 pounds; hay, 2,500 tons; beeswax, 1,250 pounds; honey, 15,000 pounds; turpentine, 600 barrels.

Factories, &c.: 1 woolen factory; 4 saw mills; 7 tar and turpentine manufactories; 4 turpentine distilleries.

Churches, 20; ministers, 10; lawyers, 7; doctors, 15; 1 female college and 6 academies, besides primary schools; post offices, 16.

This county possess great advantages in its soil, climate and natural facilities, which when combined with rail road transportation, make it very desirable to the settler.

The Wilmington, Charlotte and Rutherfordton Rail Road

runs through the heart of this county. A plank road runs to Fayetteville.

LUMBERTON is the county seat, 90 miles southeast from Raleigh.

ROCKINGHAM.

This county was organized in 1785 from Guilford, named in honor of the Marquis of Rockingham. It lies in the North western part of the State.

Surface broken and hilly.

Soil, some parts sandy, but a large part of it red clay. It produces wheat, corn, oats, buckwheat, rye, tobacco and fruits.

Area, 450 square miles.

Population, 16,500.

Farms, 800: acres improved, 111,950; unimproved, 190,500.

Natural growth of timber: ash, red, white and post oak, poplar, gum, hickory, &c.

Stock: horses, 1,859; mules, 650; cows, 2,877; other cattle, 4,000: sheep, 6,250; hogs, 16,500.

Annual products: wheat, 100,000 bushels; rye, 3,500 bushels; corn, 365,000 bushels; oats, 95,000 bushels; tobacco, 3,500,000 pounds; wool, 10,000 pounds; peas, 5,000 bushels; Irish potatoes, 15,000 bushels; sweet potatoes, 30,000 bushels; cotton, 30,000 pounds; orchard products: $5,000; wine, 1,000 gallons; butter, 88,500 pounds; hay, 500 tons; flax, 3,000 pounds; beeswax, 5,000; honey, 61,500 pounds; 40 tons of iron.

Factories, &c.: 1 cotton; 1 woolen; 25 tobacco; 5 saw mills; 15 grist mills; 2 foundries; 2 wool carding machines; 6 tanneries.

Churches, 20; ministers, 10; academies, 6; teachers, 10; lawyers, 15; doctors, 10; post offices, 15.

The lands are good, productive and pleasant. Very healthy and a desirable region. Much land can be bought on good terms.

The Greensboro and Danville Rail Road runs through this county and other Rail Roads are contemplated.

Iron, lime, and coal (bituminous) are found in this county.

WENTWORTH, the county seat, is 105 miles Northwest from Raleigh.

ROWAN.

This county was organised in 1753, from Anson.

Area, 600 square miles.

Population, 14,000.

Farms, 1,250; acres improved, 105,000; acres unimproved, 150,000.

Annual products: corn, 550,000 bushels; wheat, 95,000 bushels; oats, 150,000 bushels; potatoes, 35,000 bushels; pease, 10,000 bushels; butter, 110,000 pounds; hay, 10,000 tons; cotton, 5,000 bales.

Stock: horses, and mules, 5,000; cattle, 9,500; sheep, 7,000; hogs, 30,000.

Natural growth of forests: walnut, chestnut, oak, hickory, ash, &c.

Water courses: Yadkin River, Dutch, Third, Fourth and other creeks.

It has churches, ministers, lawyers, doctors, and teachers of high grade.

Surface generally level; soil naturally rich and productive. It produces cotton, wheat, oats and fruits in abundance. Gold and copper are found in this county, and some of its mines have been worked to great profit. Lands are low and in market.

The North Carolina Central Rail Road runs through this county.

The great Western North Carolina Extension Rail Road runs from Salisbury to the mountains.

SALISBURY is the county seat, a place of considerable trade. Population about 4,000. It is 118 miles from Raleigh.

RUTHERFORD.

A county lying in the south west part of the State, organized in 1779 out of Tyron, now extinct.

Area 870 square miles.

Population 13,550.

Farms, 1000; acres improved, 70,500; acres unimproved, 225,000.

Annual products: corn, 500,000 bushels; wheat, 30,500 bushels; oats, 85,000 bushels; potatoes, 65,220 bushels; pease, 10,330 bushels; butter, 95,500 pounds; hay, 5,000 tons; rice, 5,000 pounds; tobacco, 10,500 pounds; wool, 15,300 pounds; beeswax and honey, 15,000 pounds; 500 bales of cotton.

Stock: horses and mules, 2,700; cattle, 13,000; sheep, 10,-338; hogs, 40,000.

Natural forest: ash, elm, oak, chestnut, sugar maple, &c.

Water courses: Broad river and its tributaries run through this county.

Churches 46; several schools of different grades. Mills, &c., 25 grist mills; 7 saw mills; 10 tanneries.

Surface, broken; part mountainous.

Soil good, capable of being made highly productive. Lands are abundant and cheap, from $1 to $10. Lying as this county does along the base of the mountains makes its climate pleasant and healthy.

The Wilmington, Charlotte and Rutherford Rail Road, passes through RUTHERFORDTON, the county seat, which is about 215 miles west from Raleigh.

SAMPSON.

This county was formed in 1784, from Duplin county. It lies in the Eastern part of the State.

Area, 940 square miles.

Population, 16,500.

Farms, 1,000; acres improved, 112,000; unimproved, 365,000.

Annual products: corn, 450,000 bushels; wheat, 30,000 bushels; oats, 70,000 bushels; sweet potatoes, 265,000 bushels; pease, 10,000 bushels; butter, 105,000 pounds; hay, 5,500 tons; rice, 75,000 pounds; cotton, 2,500 bales; lumber, $20,000; turpentine, tar and pitch, about $150,000.

Natural forest: long leaf and short leaf pine, juniper, oak, hickory, &c.

Water courses: Black river, rises near the Northern boundary, and runs through the length of the county.

Churches, 28; several schools, lawyers and doctors.

Mills, &c.: grist mills, 10; tar and turpentine manufactories, 50; turpentine distilleries, 10; saw mills, 6.

Surface level; soil part sandy and rich swamps. The soil is very good for cotton, corn, oats, grapes of different kinds. Its pine lumber is valuable. The best of the land is in its original growth. Lands are cheap.

CLINTON is the county seat, and about 95 miles South of Raleigh.

STANLY.

This county was organized in 1841, and taken from Montgomery county.

Area, 280 square miles.

Population, 8,000.

Farms, 550; acres improved, 35,000; acres unimproved. 155,000.

Annual products: corn, 225,000 bushels; wheat, 35,000 bushels; oats, 30,000 bushels; potatoes, 25,000 bushels; pease, 5,500 bushels; butter, 30,500 pounds; hay, 1,500 tons; tobacco, 5,000 pounds; wool, 6,500 pounds; honey, 15,000 pounds.

Stock: horses and mules, 1,700; cattle, 5,000; sheep, 4,500; hogs, 15,000.

Natural forest: beach, elm, ash, oak, &c.

Water courses: Yadkin and Rockingham Rivers, Long Creek and others.

Gold is found in large quantities. Silver is also found in the county.

Churches, 23; several schools, lawyers and doctors. There are 10 grist mills and 8 tanneries.

This county presents great attraction for capitalists. Its water power for machinery is very great. Its mineral resources are valuable. Lands adapted to cotton, wheat, corn and fruits. They are cheap.

Albemarle is the county seat, about 140 miles from Raleigh.

STOKES.

This county was formed in 1789, out of Surry county, and lies on the Virginia line.

Area, 550 square miles.

Population, 10,500.

Farms, 650; acres improved, 35,000; unimproved 150,000.

Annual products: corn, 250,000 bushels; wheat, 20,000 bushels; oats, 50,000 bushels; potatoes, 35,000 bushels; pease, 5,000 bushels; butter, 31,000 pounds; hay, 2,000 tons; tobacco, 75,000 pounds; wool, 25,000 pounds; honey, 25,500 pounds.

Stock: horses and mules, 1,225; sheep, 5,000; cattle, 6,000; hogs, 12,000.

There are 6 iron forges; 15 grist mills; 4 saw mills; 10 tanneries; 15 tobacco factories.

Churches, 30; several ministers, lawyers and doctors, academies, schools and post offices.

Water courses: Dan river and its numerous branches run through different parts of the county.

The surface is broken and mountainous.

Soil fertile.

There are valuable deposits of iron, lime and coal in this county.

Rail Roads are projected to run through this county, which will help to develop its great natural resources. It has a healthy climate and much water power. Lands are cheap.

Danbury, is the county seat, 110 miles from Raleigh.

SURRY.

This county was organized in 1770, from Rowan county. It lies in the north western part of the State, on the Virginia line.

Area, 900 square miles.

Population, 10,500.

Farms, 1,500: acres improved, 105,000; acres unimproved, 305,000.

Annual products: corn, 155,000 bushels; wheat, 10,000 bushels; oats, 2,000 bushels; Irish Potatoes, 25,000 bushels; pease, 12,500 bushels; butter, 12,000 pounds; flax, 35,000 pounds; tobacco, 45,000 pounds; honey, 35,000 pounds.

Stock: horses and mules. 3,200; cattle, 10,500; sheep 12,000; hogs, 35,000.

Natural forests: mountain ash, poplar, chestnut, oak and hickory.

Churches, 30; 10 schools; 3 cotton factories; 10 iron forges; 2 iron founderies; 10 grist mills; 12 distilleries.

Water courses: Yadkin, Fishers and Ararat rivers and smaller creeks.

This county is mountainous, but fertile along the valleys and water courses. Lands can be bought low.

The celebrated Pilot mountain lies in the eastern part of the county. Iron ore is found in large quantities.

JEFFERSON is the county seat, about 175 miles from Raleigh.

TRANSYLVANIA.

This county was organized in 1863, out of Henderson, Haywood and Jackson.

It having been so recently organized, no official statistics have been published. It lies in the extreme South-western part of the State, in a beautitul mountain country, where corn, wheat, oats, rye, buckwheat, sorghum and clover grow luxuriantly. The finest apples are produced here in greatest perfection, as in all this western region. It is a fine grazing county.

Farms, 125: population, 4,000; churches, 22; ministers, 10; schools, 6; lawyers, 2; doctors, 8; grist mills, 20; post offices, 7.

It has vast resources in agricultural and mineral wealth to be yet developed by new settlers. Lands are cheap and abundant. The country rolling and healthy.

BREVARD is the county seat, about 220 miles from Raleigh.

TYRRELL.

This county is one of the oldest counties in the State, having been settled in 1729. It was included in what is now Washington county. It lies in the extreme eastern part of the State.

Surface level; soil good, abounding in rich swamp lands.

Area, 320 square miles.

Population, 5,000.

Farms, 300; acres improved, 21,500; acres unimproved, 163,000.

Natural growth of timber: juniper, pine, gum, oak, cypress.

Stock: horses, 428; mules, 196; cows, 1,500; other cattle, 3,500; sheep, 2,699; hogs, 8,500.

Annual products: wheat, 12,500 bushels; rye, 10,000 bushels; corn, 300,000 bushels; oats, 567 bushels; rice, 11,500 pounds; wool, 4,500 pounds; pease, 12,500 bushels; Irish potatoes, 4,300 bushels; sweet potatoes, 28,775 bushels; wine, 2,500 gallons; butter, 12,000 pounds; hay, 100 tons; flax, 4,000 pounds; beeswax, 2,500 pounds; honey, 25,000 pounds; fish, 5,000 barrels; lumber, shingles, staves, &c., $75,000.

Mills: grist mills, 2; saw mills, 4; shingle mills, 21.

Churches, 12; ministers, 4; lawyers, 1; doctors, 3; academies, 1; post offices, 2.

It is a splendid corn region and the scuppernong grape grows luxuriantly here.

The farms around Lakes Phelp are equal in soil and productiveness to any in the State.

The uncleared lands are rich and valuable for cypress lumber.

COLUMBIA is the county seat.

UNION.

This county was organized in 1842, from the Southeastern part of Mecklenburg. It lies in the Southern part of the State.

Area, 350 square miles.

Population, 11,500.

Farms, 925; acres improved, 66,500; unimproved, 236,900.

Natural growth of timber: ash, elm, beech, walnut, oak and pine.

Stock: horses, 2,163; mules, 700; cows, 3,118; other stock, 6,500; sheep, 11,641; hogs, 20,500.

Annual products; wheat, 76,321 bushels; corn, 305,000 bushels; oats, 26,000 bushels; tobacco, 5,000 pounds; cotton, 4,500 bales; wool, 14,000 pounds; pease, 18,500 bushels; Irish potatoes, 7,500 bushels; sweet potatoes, 35,000 bushels; orchard products, $5,000; market vegetables, $6,500; butter, 85,476 pounds; hay, 500 tons; maple molasses, 1,500 gallons; honey, 32,000 pounds.

Churches, 23; ministers, 10; academies, 2; primary schools,

4; teachers, 10; lawyers 2; doctors, 9; post offices, 10; grist mills, 20.

Mines: 6 gold mines located in the Northwestern part of the countr.

Water courses: Rocky river, Crooked, Richard's, Negro Head, Lane and Wraxhaw creeks.

This county is rich in minerals, especially in gold. Solid lumps have been found, worth from $2,000 to $3,000, and there is but little doubt that the mines are very rich.

The soil is very productive for grain of all kinds, and may be bought at low prices.

This county was the birth place of Andrew Jackson, President of the United States.

Granite underlies a part of the surface, and extensive beds of slate are found in other parts. The whetstone is found near Monroe.

MONROE is the county seat, 150 miles Southwest from Raleigh.

WAKE.

This county was organized in 1790, and named after Gov. Tyron's wife. It is beautifully located in the centre of the State.

Area, 950 square miles.

Population, 26,000.

Farms, 1,500; acres improved, 185,000; unimproved, 368,000; cash value of land, $3,500,000.

Stock: horses, 4,000; mules, 1,235; cows, 5,639; other cattle, 11,000; sheep, 10,750; hogs, 50,000.

Annual products: wheat, 80,000 bushels; corn, 750,000 bushels; cotton, 5,000 bales; rice, 13,000 pounds; wool, 14,000 pounds; pease, 50,000 bushels; Irish potatoes, 15,000 bushels; sweet potatoes, 250,000 bushels; orchard products, $1,500; market vegetables, $10,000; butter 150,000 pounds; hay, 10,000 tons; beeswax, 2,000 pounds; honey, 40,000.

Churches, 40; 1 male College at Wake Forest; academies, 10, and primary schools; ministers, 70; teachers, 50; lawyers, 25; doctors, 40.

There is one paper mill, 1 foundry and machine shop, 1 foundery and plow factory, 1 sash and planing factory, 10 steam saw mills and 40 grist mills.

Water courses: Neuse river runs through the county, Swift, Walnut, Crabtree, New Light and Big lick creeks.

The North Carolina Central Rail Road runs through the

county. The Raleigh & Gaston Rail Road also runs from Raleigh to Weldon. A Rail Road is in progress from Raleigh to be extended through the Coalfields in Chatham to Columbia, South Carolina.

This county produces tobacco, corn, oats, cotton, sorghum, pease, potatoes, fruits and garden vegetables in great abundance. Lands are cheap and it is a very desirable section for the emigrant.

There is a large mine of plumbago within a few miles of Raleigh, that has been largely worked. Granite also abounds in various places.

RALEIGH is the capital of the State and seat of justice for Wake county. It is a growing city and a desirable and healthy place. The public institutions of the State are located here: the Institution for the Deaf, Dumb and the Blind, the Lunatic Asylum and the Penitentiary.

WARREN.

This county was organized in 1779, from an old county (Bute) now extinct. It lies in the northern part of the State and borders upon Virginia.

Area, 480 square miles.

Population, 13,765.

Farms, 600; acres improved, 122,000; acres unimproved, 225,500.

Natural growth of timber: oak, hickory, walnut, ash, elm, cedar, gum, &c.

Stock: horses, 3,964; mules, 900; cows, 3,500; other cattle, 6,500; sheep, 7,500; hogs, 25,000.

Annual Products: wheat, 125,000 bushels; corn, 500,000 bushels; oats, 98,000 bushels; tobacco, 6,150,000 pounds; cotton 500 bales; wool, 13,500 pounds; pease, 50,000 bushels; Irish potatoes, 15,000 bushels; sweet potatoes, 66,500 bushels; butter, 65,842 pounds; hay, 3,500 tons; beeswax, 1,200 pounds; honey, 15,000 pounds.

There are 22 churches; 15 ministers; academies: 2 female and 4 others; teachers, 15; lawyers, 6; doctors, 15; merchants, 25; post offices, 11.

There are 21 grist mills; 4 saw mills; 3 distilleries; 6 tanneries.

It is watered by Roanoke River, Nutbush, Fishing and Shocco Creeks.

This county is considered one of the best in the State. The people are intelligent and hospitable. Lands are fertile, rich and productive.

It is intersected by the Raleigh and Gaston Rail Road.

WARRENTON, the county seat, 63 miles west from Raleigh, about 4 miles south from the Raleigh and Gaston Rail Road.

Ridgeway is well located on the Raleigh and Gaston Rail Road, and quite a town is springing up here, with vineyards, orchards and market gardens all around it.

WASHINGTON.

This county was organized in 1799, and named after Gen. George Washington.

Surface, level; soil rich and productive.

Area, 400 square miles.

Population, 6,500.

Farms, 500; acres improved, 25,000; acres unimproved, 75,000.

Natural growth of timber: oak, elm, pine, juniper, cedar, gum and cypress.

Stock: horses, 675; mules, 250, cows, 1,500; other stock, 3,000; sheep, 2,500; hogs, 10,000.

Annual products: wheat, 35,750 bushels; oats, 2,000 bushels; corn, 250,000 bushels; rye, 1,000 bushels; rice, 10,000 pounds; wool, 5,000 pounds; pease, 20,000 bushels; Irish potatoes, 7,000 bushels; sweet potatoes, 50,000 bushels; hay, 2,000 tons; 20,000 barrels of tar and turpentine; $30,000 worth of lumber; 5,000 barrels of fish, besides grapes, wine, apples, &c.

There are churches, 15; ministers, 10; academies and schools, 6; lawyers, 4; doctors, 6; teachers, 8; post offices, 4.

There are 20 tar and turpentine manufactories, 3 grist mills, 6 shingle mills, 1 ship yard.

Water courses: Roanoke River and Welch Creek on the west, Albemarle Sound on the north. Scuppernong River and Lake Phelps on the east, and Lake Pungo on the south.

This is one of the prettiest counties in the east. Lying on the Albemarle Sound.

There is in this county, in its natural growth, lands that will, when brought into cultivation, be as rich and valuable as any in the State. Its land, lumber, fisheries and productions, with easy access to all parts of the United States give it peculiar advantages and attractions.

PLYMOUTH is the county seat, 162 miles east from Raleigh.

WATAUGA.

This county was organized in 1849, from Ashe, Caldwell, Wilkes and Yancey, deriving its name from an Indian river. It lies in the Northwestern part of the State.

Surface, mountainous.

Soil, fertile.

Area, 500 square miles.

Population 5,000

Farms, 500; acres improved, 25,000; unimproved, 145,000.

Stock: horses, 850; mules, 155; cows, 1,607; other cattle, 3,000; sheep, 6,000; hogs, 12,500.

Annual products: wheat, 14,000 bushels; rye, 13,800 bushels; corn, 110,000 bushels; oats, 40,500 bushels; rice 1,000 pounds; tobacco, 10,000 pounds; cotton, 500 bales; wool, 12,000 pounds; pease, 10,500 bushels; Irish potatoes, 20,000 bushels; sweet potatoes, 1,500 bushels; buckwheat, 10,000 bushels; orchard produce, $12,565; market gardening, $13,410; butter 75,000 pounds; cheese, 5,000 pounds; hay, 4,500 tons; fiax, 25,000 pounds; maple sugar, 15,000 pounds; maple molasses, 6,000 gallons; beeswax, 1,500 pounds; honey, 20,000 pounds

Churches, 12; ministers, 8; academies and primary schools, 10; lawyers, 1; doctors, 3; grist mill, 10; post offices, 8.

Natural growth of timber: sugar maple, elm, oak, ash, pine, &c.

Water courses: New river, Watauga river, Elk, Cau, Neal, Camp and other creeks.

This county lying off the line of travel and commerce, has not been able to develop its resources, like many others, but when its mines are worked, its lands cultivated, with its stock raising advantages, &c., and its mountain scenery, it will be very desirable.

Good land from fifty cents per acre to five dollars are found in this county.

BOONE, the county seat, is 240 miles West from Raleigh. It was named after Daniel Boone, the celebrated hunter.

WAYNE.

This county was organized in 1779, from Dobb's county, now extinct. It lies in the Eastern part of the State.

Surface level; soil excellent.

Population 15,000.

Area, 450 square miles.

Acres improved, 109,000; unimproved, 200,000; cash value of land, $3,500,000.

Stock: horses, 2,225; mules, 500; cows, 2,500; other cattle, 4,500; sheep, 4,000; hogs, 40,000.

Annual products: wheat, 16,650 bushels; rye, 20,000 bushels; corn, 550,000 bushels; oats, 15,000 bushels; rice, 10,000 pounds, cotton, 6,000 bales; pease, 110,000 bushels; Irish potatoes, 10,000 bushels; sweet potatoes, 175,000 bushels; orchard products, $10,500; wine, 1,000 gallons; butter, 35,000 pounds; hay, 5,000 tons; honey, 15,000 pounds; turpentine, tar and lumber, $100,000.

Churches, 25; ministers, 15; female colleges, 1; academies, 4; primary schools, 10; lawyers, 7; doctors, 10; post offices, 10; saw mills, 6; grist mills, 8; tar and turpentine manufactories, 51; turpentine distilleries, 10

Water courses: Neuse river, Little river, Nahunta, Falling and Sleepy Creeks.

Native Forest: pine, oak, ash, gum, &c.

The lands on Neuse river, Little river and their tributaries are very rich and productive.

Corn, cotton, wheat, oats, sugar cane, fruits and vegetables are productive here abundantly. Its facilities for traveling and exportation by water and Rail Roads are very good. It is, perhaps, second to Edgecombe as a cotton growing county, and is very desirable for truck farming and vineyards.

The North Carolina Central Rail Road, the North Carolina Atlantic Rail Road, and the Wilmington & Weldon Rail Road all centre and cross the county at Goldsboro. Much good land for sale on easy terms. This is a first rate county for immigrants.

GOLDSBORO is the county seat, a growing place. It is fifty miles East from Raleigh, eighty-four miles North from Wilmington, seventy-eight miles South from Weldon, sixty miles from New Bern, and ninety-five miles from Morehead City.

WILKES.

This county was organized in 1777, from Surry, and named after John Wilkes, the English statesman.

Wilkes county lies in the north-western part of the State.

Area, 550 square miles.

Population, 15,000.

Farms, 1,125; acres improved, 75,000; acres unimproved, 270,000.

Natural growth of timber: white ash, sugar maple, beech, oak, gum, &c.

Stock: horses, 2,362; mules, 300; cows, 3,000; other cattle, 5,000; sheep, 7,874; hogs, 25,000.

Annual products: wheat, 55,566 bushels; rye, 12,000 bushels; corn, 310,000 bushels; oats, 36,566 bushels; tobacco, 100,000 pounds; wool, 15,877 pounds; pease, 10,000 bushels; Irish potatoes, 15,000 bushels; sweet potatoes, 27,000 bushels; orchard products, $30,000; wine, 500 gallons; butter, 85,000 pounds; hay, 500 bales; cheese, 3,000 pounds; flax, 18,000 pounds; flaxseed, 2,000 pounds; sorghum molasses, 5,500 gallons; beeswax, 36,000 pounds; honey, 75,000 pounds; home manufactures, $36,000.

There are churches, 48; ministers, 20; academies and primary schools, 12; teachers, 15; lawyers, 4; doctors, 10; post offices, 10.

Factories: cotton factory, 1; linseed oil mill, 1; tanneries, 8; grist mills, 12.

Water courses: Yadkin River and Reddie River, Moravian, Lewis Fork, Roaring, Mulberry, Bugaboo, Elkin and Cub Creeks.

Mountains: it is nearly surrounded by the Ridge and spurs of the Blue Ridge.

It is thought there are extensive beds of iron ore in the northern part of the county.

Lands are very cheap and abundant. On the water courses the lands are very good. Corn, wheat, rye, oats, tobacco and fruits grow well here. There is an abundance of water power for manufactories.

WILKESBORO' is the county seat, 172 miles north-west from Raleigh.

WILSON.

This county was organized in 1856, and named after Gen. Wilson of Edgecombe, who died at Vera Cruz in Mexico, during the war with Mexico.

Area, 250 square miles.

Population 9,750.

Farms, ——; acres improved, 65,000; acres unimproved, 115,500. Cash value $1,500,000.

Native forests: pine, oak, hickory, ash, &c.

Stock: horses, 1,200; mules, 600; cows, 1,280; other cattle, 3,000; sheep, 2,725; hogs, 20,591.

Annual products: wheat, 5,000 bushels; rye, 12,000 bushels; corn, 230,000 bushels; oats, 4,500 bushels; cotton, 3,500 bales; wool, 5,000 pounds; pease, 5,000 bushels; Irish potatoes, 8,000 bushels; sweet potatoes, 75,000 bushels; orchard products, $5,000; wine, 1,000 gallons; butter, 10,000 pounds; hay, 3,000 tons; honey, 10,000 pounds.

Churches, 15; ministers, 10; 4 academies; 6 primary schools; teachers, 12; lawyers, 7; doctors, 10; post offices, 6.

There are 8 grist mills; 4 steam saw mills; 25 tar and turpentine manufactories.

Natural growth: pine, oak, gum, cypress, &c.

This county contains much fine land. It produces well, cotton, corn wheat, oats, potatoes, pease, grapes, apples, peaches and other fruits. It is well adapted to grape raising.

Good land can be bought on good terms and fair prices.

The Wilmington and Weldon Rail Road runs through this county.

WILSON is the county seat, situated on the Wilmington and Weldon Rail Road, 48 miles east from Raleigh.

YANCEY.

This county was organized in 1833, from Buncombe. It lies on the North-western line of the State, and bounded on the West by the State of Tennessee.

Surface generally mountainous. Soil productive.

Area, 680 square miles.

Population, 8,655.

Farms, 970; acres improved, 46,000; acres unimproved, 265,675.

Natural growth of timber: black oak, white oak, red oak, chestnut oak, poplar, sugar maple, mountain birch, mahogany, walnut, cherry, locust, persimmon, balsam, pine and numerous others, of small growth.

Stock: horses, 1,674; mules, 300; cows, 3,000; other cattle, 4,507; sheep, 6,500; hogs, 25,500.

Annual products: wheat, 40,000 bushels; rye, 6500 bushels; corn, 25,000 bushels; oats, 60,500 bushels; tobacco, 20,000 pounds; wool, 15,000 pounds; sweet potatoes, 50,000 bushels.

There are 20 ministers, 10 academies, 4 primary schools, 20 teachers, 2 lawyers, 5 doctors, 5 post offices, 13 grist mills, 6 tanneries, &c.

Mines: gold, copper, silver, iron, copperas and black lead are found in the mines of Fork Creek, South Yoe river, Egypt, Caney river and other parts of the county.

The soil generally is highly productive and produces luxuriant crops of tobacco, wheat, oats, buckwheat, butter, honey and fruit.

Cattle can be raised in any quantity.

Orchards can be made to any extent. Apples have been grown in this county weighing a pound and a-half.

Its water courses are, Nalychucky river, Caney river and Yoe river, Pigeon and Cat tail creeks.

Here is the range of the celebrated Black mountain, being the highest range of mountains in the United States, east of the Rocky mountains. The sides and tops are covered with the balsam tree, the highest peak is called Mitchells peak.

BURNSVILLE is the county seat, 240 miles north-west from Raleigh.

YADKIN.

This county was organized in 1850, from the southern part of Surry, deriving its name from the Yadkin river.

Area, 310 square miles.

Population, 10,900.

Acres improved, 62,000; acres unimproved, 138,000. Cash value, $1,125,000.

Natural growth of timber: mountain ash, gum, chestnut, oak, &c.

Stock: horses, 1,796; mules, 500; cows, 2,000; other cattle, 3,000; sheep, 6,000; hogs, 16,225.

Annual products: wheat, 67,810 bushels; rye, 6,866 bushels; corn, 300,000 bushels; oats, 50,000 bushels; tobacco, 155,542 pounds; wool, 10,000 pounds; Irish potatoes, 8,000 bushels; sweet potatoes, 20,000 bushels; orchard products $15,500; butter, 70,000 pounds; cheese, 3,250 pounds; hay, 1,500 tons; flax, 6,500 pounds; flax seed, 2,000 pounds; sorghum molasses, 3,000 gallons; beeswax, 5,000 pounds; honey, 70,000 pounds.

There are churches, 25; ministers, 15; academies, 4; primary schools, 8; teachers, 15; lawyers, 3; doctors, 16; post offices, 10.

There are 15 grist mills; 3 saw mills, &c.

Water courses: Yadkin rivèr forms the north and east boundary of the county. Deep creek and Panther creek with their branches spread nearly all over the county.

This a splendid county for settlers, good churches and schools, healthy climate, good farming land and can be purchased on good terms.

YADKINVILLE the county seat, 130 miles north west from Raleigh.

CORRESPONDENCE.

In order to obtain the latest and most reliable information, both general and specific, in regard to the agricultural, mining and manufacturing resources of North Carolina, the general character of its soils, climate, productiveness, and prices of lands, the North Carolina Land Company requested several intelligent and prominent gentlemen of the State to furnish that information. The following letters is the result of that request.

The reader will find much valuable matter in these letters, from the most undoubted sources, and will find the labor of reading them both pleasant and instructive.

The first letter we present, is a most valuable contribution from Hon. Wm. B. Rodman, an intelligent native and long resident of the State, an able lawyer and a practical farmer, and one of the Judges of the Supreme Court of the State. Mr. R. is a resident of Washington, Beaufort Co., but writes from this city while in attendance here upon official duties:

RALEIGH, April 2, 1869.

To the North Carolina Land Company:

GENTLEMEN :

For the purposes of physical geography, the State of North Carolina may be divided by lines running nearly northeast and southwest, and somewhat parallel to each other, into four belts or sections. The first of these, is bounded by the ocean on the east, by the State of Virginia on the north and on the west by a line beginning on the line between Virginia and North Carolina north of the western border of Perquimans county, about 76 deg. 20 m. longitude west of Greenwich, and running thence in a southeastern course to Wilmington on the Cape Fear river. This may be called the swamp land section: it comprises the following counties: Currituck, Camden, Pasquotank, Perquimans, Chowan, Washington, Tyrrell, Beaufort, Hyde,

Craven, Carteret, Jones, Onslow, New Hanover and Brunswick.

The other sections may be briefly defined as follows:

Second section, or cotton region: west of the former, and bounded on the west, beginning at the falls of the Roanoke at Weldon and running in a general southwestern direction to the western boundary of Richmond county.

Third section, which may be called the central one, extending from the western boundary of the second, to the foot of the mountains.

Fourth section, which may be called the mountain one, to the western boundary of the State.

The climate, soil and productions of these sections considerably differ. It is to the first of these sections alone, that this letter is devoted.

Physical Geography of the Swamp Land Belt—The Banks.

It will be seen from a map, that the extreme eastern limit of the State, consists of a narrow strip of land extending along the entire coast, and separating the ocean from the interior waters. This strip is sandy, varying in width from about one-fourth of a mile, to about five miles: in places it is entirely bare of vegetation being merely the beach of the ocean: in other places, especially in the neighborhood of Cape Hatteras, where it is widest, it is covered by live oaks, red cedars and the ordinary trees of the main land, and a shrub called yeopon, from which is made a tea much valued by some. This strip of land is called the Banks. It is broken only by four considerable inlets, Hatteras, Ocracoke, Beaufort and at the mouth of the Cape Fear river. Through these, vessels from the sea enter the interior waters. The depth of water which can be carried into the interior through Hatteras or Ocracoke is eight feet, at Beaufort sixteen, at the mouth of the Cape Fear twelve. This strip of land is not suited to agriculture; the frequent winds prevent the cultivation of the grains or of any, but low growing vegetables, but the soil is not in most places barren; and the melons and sweet potatoes grown on the banks, are considered to have more saccharine matter, than those of the interior. It is pretty thickly populated, the people live by fishing and pilotage. A peculiar breed of ponies is raised on the marshes connected with the Banks. During the whole year they live on the grass of the salt marshes, and are never stabled or fed with grain. As this country is not inviting to emigration, we pass it over with this very brief description.

The Sounds.

Commencing just south of the Virginia line, the water separating the Banks from the main land. is called Currituck sound. It varies in width from three to fifteen miles; the water is fresh or only brackish; it is nearly every where shallow, and abounds with small marshy islands. It abounds with fish, and during the winter is resorted to, by immense quantities of wild ducks, geese and swans, great numbers of which are annually killed by sportsmen and sold at high prices in the Northern cities. These fowls are also found numerously, but in less abundance, feeding along the shores of all the sounds and rivers. The marshes from their advantages for shooting them, have a pecuniary value, which they would not otherwise have, and are sometimes rented out to amateurs and others at fancy prices.

Albermarle sound is a large sheet of fresh or brackish water, from eight to thirty miles wide, into which flow the Roanoke, Chowan and other smaller rivers, that will be elsewhere described. Immense quantities of herrings, shad, bass and other fish are caught every spring on the shores of this sound and the rivers emptying into it, by long seines and in gill nets.

Croatan sound connects Albemarle with Pamlico sound; this latter is always salt—it is about thirty miles wide from east to west and has from eight to ten feet of water. Core sound about three miles wide, and with a channel of five feet depth, connects Pamlico sound with Beaufort inlet, at the town of Beaufort and Morehead city.

The harbor at Beaufort is one of the best on the Atlantic coast, south of Norfolk. Vessels drawing sixteen feet can enter at any time, and discharge their cargoes at the pier of the Atlantic and North Carolina Railroad Company. It will in the future be the site of an important city.

Rivers and Creeks.

This whole country is well watered; there is no part of it more than ten miles from navigable water, and much the greater part is much nearer. The Chowan river is navigable by eight feet water into Virginia—a regular line of steamboats runs every other day up this and the Blackwater river, (one of its branches) and at Franklin connects with the Roanoke and Seaboard Railroad, running to Norfolk. Frequent steamboats also, ply from Hamilton which may be considered the head of navigation on the Roanoke river, and from the towns and landings lower down the river, through two canals which connect Albemarle sound with the Elizabeth river at Norfolk. Boats drawing six feet water navigate these canals.

Tar river, (so called in its upper course, but called Pamlico river in its course below Willow Point two miles above the town of Washington,) is the next considerable river south of the Roanoke. It is six miles wide at its mouth, and navigable by vessels drawing eight feet water, to the town of Washington thirty miles from its mouth; by boats drawing two feet, to Greenville twenty-five miles higher up, during the whole year; and to Tarboro, twenty-five miles above Greenville, for about nine months in the year. The climate and soil of the valley of the Tar river from its mouth to its source is the finest and most productive in the State.

Going south we come to Neuse river, another noble stream, nine miles wide at its mouth, having the same depth of water as the Pamlico, up to New Berne about thirty miles from its mouth, and navigable by small steamers during the greater part of the year, some fifty miles higher up.

The Cape Fear is also a noble stream, having twelve feet water to Wilmington thirty-two miles, and navigable by small steamers to Fayetteville about eighty miles higher up.

The Mainland—Its Soil.

The section which we are now describing is alike in its main physical features throughout. The part immediately bordering on the sounds to the east, is but little elevated above mean tide, but there is a general, nearly uniform, ascent of from one to two feet per mile towards the northwest. This is not universally true: on the banks of the rivers bluffs of from twenty to thirty feet high are occasionally found, and the land is sometimes slightly rolling and broken. Between each of the rivers, there is an elevation parallel to their general course, but always being a good deal nearer the northern, than the southern stream: on a line from Washington to Plymouth this elevation is forty feet; between Washington and New Berne it is probably about twenty five or thirty feet. Probably six-tenths of the country consists of what are called swamp or poccosin lands. It is important to just ideas, that the meaning of the word "swamp," in this connection, should not be misunderstood. It does not mean, that the lands are at any time submerged by the tides or freshets: on the contrary, much of the swamp is higher than what is called the high land. In order to understand it, we may assume, as is the fact, that at a very recent period speaking geologically, the section we are describing, and also the section above it, as high up as the falls of the rivers, was a shallow sound of salt water, like those which now skirt the coast, the present surface exactly resembled the present bottoms of those sounds, where we find occasional sandy shoals or ridges thrown up by the currents, enclosing more or less completely, small or large spaces of water several feet deeper, in which the finer sediment brought down by the rivers settles, mixed with shells and other remains of fishes. The land was gradually elevated by a force acting from the northwest; the shoals being elevated above the water, but the deeper enclosed places continuing, probably for a long time, to form shallow lakes: these have gradually filled up, by the wash from the neighboring lands, and by the decay of the luxuriant vegetation which they have produced for ages. These former lakes are the swamp lands; they have all an abundant elevation for drainage: and during much of the summer are dry. There are two reasons why the rain which falls on them, does not run off fast enough to admit of their cultivation in their natural state. 1st. There is almost always a narrow strip of land, higher by two or three feet, than the contiguous edge of the swamp, lying between the lower portion of it, and the nearest water course; and the branches which are found intersecting this strip, have been so filled up by matter washed in, and by a profuse growth of trees, bushes and reeds, as to be inadequate to discharge the amount of water pressing towards them. 2nd. The whole surface is always covered with a dense growth of trees or shrubbery, through which the water can find its way but very slowly. It is necessary therefore, to enlarge and deepen these natural drains, before undertaking to clear the land for cultivation.

These swamps now produce, in varying quantities, the most valuable timber trees: cypress, white cedar or juniper, poplar, swamp pine and various kinds of oak, besides gums, maples, &c., of less value. Some of these trees are of immense size: cypress and poplars are found over five feet in diameter at four feet above the ground. A single cypress will sometimes make shingles worth $100. The soil generally consists, for two or more feet, of sand and clay extremely comminuted, and of decayed vegetable matter in varying proportions; below this is very often found a bed of oyster or other shells, or possibly a blue sand of a foot or more thickness, and then a somewhat tenacious clay. When well drained, it is of great and enduring fertility, producing per acre from thirty to fifty bushels of Indian corn, or from 400 to 600 pounds ginned cotton, or from ten to twenty bushels of wheat, or other crops in like proportion. There are fields in Hyde county which have been cultivated 100 years without rest or manure, and they may now be relied on for thirty-five bushels of corn per acre.

The price of lands depends so much on circumstances, which are hardly ever the same in any two instances, that it is difficult to give any scale which would be reliable by a stranger. In the county of Beaufort in 1860, an ordinary piece of swamp land, not more than a mile from a water course, or from boat navigation, unimproved in any way, would readily sell for from five to ten dollars per acre. With less advantages the prices would be less. The prices were about the same in other counties. At this time such land, when drained and in good condition for cultivation, is usually rented out at five dollars per acre, or for one-third of the corn, or one-fourth of the cotton crop.

The high lands have already been partially described as forming ridges separating the swamps, and obstructing the discharge of their waters; they vary in width, from a few yards to several miles, and in composition, from a light sand to a stiff clay. They also require drainage, but not as much as the swamps; they are generally, in their original state covered with beautiful groves of long leaf pine and occasional oaks. They were usually worth when unimproved about one-half as much as the swamps, the general situation being the same. They would produce with the same cultivation rather less than one-half as much. Many persons, however, prefer them to the swamps for cotton, as when marled they produce a better staple, and the crops ripen earlier.

In the counties of this section probably not over one-tenth of the land is cleared.

Climate and Staple Productions.

The section we have been describing lies between thirty-seven and thirty-four degrees of North latitude. Of course the summers are longer, and the winters milder in the southern than in the northern part. No where does the snow ever lie on the ground more than a few days; at Wilmington it is rarely seen. The climate is warmest in winter and coolest in summer, nearest the coast. At Hatteras the Palmetto grows, which elsewhere is not found north of Charleston; this is owing to the proximity of the gulf stream. North of Albemarle sound cotton is not much grown as a staple crop. South of that it, with Indian corn, is the main crop. This section and the one just West of it, is probably unsurpassed in the world as a cotton growing country. It is conceded that on the choice lands of Alabama, Louisiana, &c , larger crops can be *sometimes* made than it is possible to make in North Carolina. But in those States there is an uncertainty and a liability to accidents, such as inundations, boll worm, army worm, &c., &c., which do not attach to this favored region; and it is the opinion of many intelligent men who have planted in both sections, that on an average of ten years the crops of these sections of North Carolina would exceed those of the most fertile portions of the Southwest.

Health.

Like all countries with an alluvial soil, chills and fever are the most common forms of disease; bilious fever also occurs sometimes in August and September, but the country is in general eminently salubrious. Consumption, unless imported is entirely unknown. The longevity of this section is equal to that of any in the United States. The census of 1860 shows the average mortality of the whole United States for that year to have been 127 in 10,000, and the average mortality of a tier of two counties next to the Atlantic, from Delaware to Florida inclusive, was 134 in 10,000. When it is considered that in this were included the unhealthy coasts of South Carolina and Florida, we must conclude that the mortality of the North Carolina portion of this district, was less than the average. The mortality in Massachusetts was 176 in the 10,000. Contrary to what might perhaps have been expected, the swamp lands are the healthiest, and those immediately on the banks of the rivers, the least so. This may be accounted for by the more sudden changes of temperature arising from greater exposure to the ocean winds, rapid cooling and catching cold.

Fruits.

Every part of this section is well adapted to raising apples, pears, peaches, figs, pomegranates, quinces, blackberries and raspberries, and the swamp lands to cranberries and strawberries. The Catawba, Isabella and other grapes grow well, but the peculiar and most valuable grape of this belt is the Scuppernong: it is about the size of a boy's marble, of a dark purple, or a transparent yellowish green color; it grows singly, not in bunches; ripens in August and Sept. It is propagated by layers, never pruned, runs on arbors, bears in three years from the planting, and in five years will cover a space of 100 square feet and bear over two bushels to the vine. All who are acquainted with its excellencies, esteem it above all others as a table grape, and by general consent it makes the best wine made in the United States. One bushel of grapes will make from four to seven gallons of wine, which is worth four dollars per gallon. The manufacture of wine is assuming large proportions. The raising of vegetables to ship through Norfolk, to New York, is an established and profitable business. The seasons, it is computed, are about one week earlier for every half degree of latitude one goes South, but proximity to the sea, or a location on the south side of a wide water course, has much influence in this respect.

Cattle.

The climate is favorable to the raising of all domesticated animals. Horses and mules thrive. Cattle keep fat on the native wild grasses for nine months in the year, and many never receive grain or hay or shelter, during the whole year. Hogs could keep fat all the year in the swamps on acorns and reed roots, but during the summer they are liable to be killed by bears. Sheep require an open country and attention to protect the lambs from wild cats.

Game.

Deer and hares, abound; there are plenty of foxes for the amusement of sportsmen. Quail and other birds are numerous. The finest fish are plentiful and cheap.

Population.

The numbers of the people will be given under the heads of the several counties; the country will easily support twenty times its present numbers. The people are kind, honest, peaceable, and not very industrious or enterprising. In no country is there more disposition to welcome and assist all worthy immigrants, whether they come with or without means. Crimes of violence are extremely rare—the laws are fairly administered.

Internal Improvements.

The State has done but little in the way of artificial improvement for this part of its territory. The two canals connecting Albemarle sound with Norfolk have been already spoken of. In 1840 the State cut two canals connecting Pungo lake and Alligator lake with Pungo river. Navigation is everywhere so convenient that railroads are not absolutely needed for local purposes. It is probable, however that the necessity of a speedier and more direct communication, between the thriving cities of Norfolk and the North, and Wilmington and the further South, will soon compel the construction of a railroad from Norfolk or Suffolk to Edenton, thence it will be connected by a line of steamboats with Plymouth, and from thence the road will run through Washington and New Berne to Wilmington, thus shortening the communication between the Northern and Southern Atlantic cities by over 100 miles, and opening to a country, admirably adapted to the raising of fruits and vegetables, the markets of the great cities.

Very Respectfully,
WM. B. RODMAN.

The following letter is from the pen of Rev. W. E. Pell, a well known clergyman and native of the State, and recently the able editor of the *Sentinel*, a leading newspaper, whose long and extensive acquaintance with almost every portion of the State, enables him to furnish an array of facts, which are of the highest interest to the emigrant.

RALEIGH, N. C. *April* 4, 1869.

To the President and Directors of the North Carolina Land Company:

GENTLEMEN:—Every philanthropist at all interested in the future welfare of the toiling millions of Europe and of our own Northern States, and every well-wisher to the real and permanent interests of North Carolina, must thank you for the intelligent, enterprising and well-directed efforts you are making, to induce emigrants from those crowded and over taxed sections, to seek a home in the Old North State.

For many years, when I have instituted a comparison between the cheap, productive lands of the South, and especially of this State, their accessibility to market, their large returns to skilled and intelligent labor, their varied products and the superiority of our climate for health and enjoyment, to the high-priced lands of the Northwest, the enormous cost of transportation for the heavy products of that section, the short term allowed for labor in that cold bleak region, and the little prospect of acquiring in that section wealth or a competency for old age from the labors of the farm, I have been astonished at the steady and enormous increase of population in those States, and the very small accessions from emigration to the population of the Southern States.

Can this fact be explained upon any sound principle, conceding that the emigrants themselves know what they are about? I think not. I must conclude, therefore, that large bodies of emigrants to the North-west, both from the Northern and Eastern States and from Europe, are either ignorant of the superiority of the advantages we possess in the South, or that they are the dupes of designing men and their agents, who are largely interested in the sale of Western lands and in Rail Roads; or that while Northern men and Europeans alike declare their freedom from all prejudices against *race or color*, they are, nevertheless, the subjects of that very prejudice, which leads them to eschew all contact with the *black race.* If this latter reason has heretofore influenced their action, it ought not longer to exist, since the laws of these Southern States as well as the laws of the United States, have removed all grounds for this prejudice, by declaring that the *negro* is to all intents and purposes, the full brother and equal of the *white man!*

Believing that this rush of immigration to the far-west is the result of ignorance on the part of the emigrant, or the cupidity and deception of the land speculators, and Rail Road corporations, I readily comply with your request, to furnish you with the facts and reasons, which go to prove unmistakably, that North Carolina is a better home for the emigrant, than the North-west.

ADVANTAGE ARISING FROM OCCUPATION AND IMPROVEMENT.

The region in the Northwest most inviting to the foreign emigrant or the Northern and Eastern settler, or to which their eyes are most earnestly directed by the Agents of the land speculators in New York and other places, *is chiefly a new country*, from which the Indians have been recently expelled and which is still the haunt of wild beasts,—open praries or wild forests, with but few civilized inhabitants. Here, nature in its wildest forms holds possession. The forests are unfelled, cultivation is yet in its infancy and only in patches; none but the rudest tenements, if any, for human dwellings exist; the lands unfenced, if opened, and every thing for shelter, for comfort and support must *be begun.* No churches, no schools, no forges, no machine shops, no mills, no physicians, no domestic animals, no laws but such as are *improvised* for the immediate wants of the settlement, to exert their controlling or conservative influence. Life in fact must be begun afresh, in new and in many of its most trying forms. Or if they are directed to the untenanted lands of Indiana, Illinois,

Michigan, Minnesota, Wisconsin, Iowa, or Missouri, here the immigrant finds a stirring population, too much in earnest to make money to be hospitable to the stranger, brim full of the idea of speculation or of reprisals upon the new settler, in the shape of high prices for lands, and every article he is obliged to purchase; while as yet the meagre supply of mills, stores, machines, schools, churches, &c., render them almost inaccessible to the means and wants of the settler.

In North Carolina the case is totally different. In the older portions of the State, lands, tenements, mills, stores, physicians, schools and churches are generally within the reach of almost any number of new settlers. Persons with slender means who come into the State to settle, are not advised to plunge into the extensive, uncultivated forests which abound more or less in all parts of the State, but especially in the western counties, or into the unreclaimed swamp lands of the East. The rapid increase of the negro population in the South during the existence of slavery, and the intense thirst for money-making among the whites, together with the remarkable cheapness of the lands, seemed to render the annual clearing of new lands necessary. The consequence was that every large slave-owner cut down and opened a new farm every year, and as soon as the lands were a little worn, instead of improving them with manure, (a much cheaper and easier and a more sensible process than cutting down new lands) they were abandoned or turned out, to enable the planter to cultivate his fresher fields.

What is the result? Why since the abolition of slavery and the reduction of the field labor of the South by one half, by the withdrawal of many strong laborers, and of the negro women, boys and girls, from the tillage of the soil, there are in North Carolina perhaps one half of the lands formerly tilled in the State, that are now uncultivated. Much of the lands regarded formerly as worn out, have grown up in pine, which now are easily cleared, and by rest have vastly improved. Many of these lands are capable of the highest improvement and may be bought very low. Besides this there are thousands of acres of cleared land, with tenements of various kinds upon them, scattered from the sea-board to the mountains, but especially in the Eastern Counties, which invite the settler, at very low rates. These are in the midst of a peaceable, hospitable and law abiding people, surrounded with schools, churches, factories, stores, mechanic shops, physicians, mills and all the appurtenances of civilized life. How much better this, when things are equal, to the wild, unsettled, uncivilized condition of the Northwest to which immigration is now rushing? I do not over-state the case when I say, that there are this day, untenanted open lands enough in North

Carolina, to settle comfortably by the 1st of January 1870, in time for the making of the next crop, 200,000 new settlers, cheaper and better adapted to the purposes of comfort, wealth and happiness, than the new, cold, inhospitable country to which new settlers are directed in the Northwest.

But again, an examination of the statistics of the several counties of the State, will show, that not one-third of the lands of North Carolina to this day are opened—they remain in their native upland or swampy forests, covering much of the very best lands of the State, from which the wild beasts have been nearly expelled. Large portions of these lands lie in bodies of from five thousand to one hundred thousand acres, suited to the settlement of colonies

ADVANTAGE IN VARIETY OF CROPS.

It will be seen, that I present considerations intended especially to direct the movements of the emigrant who is or intends to be a cultivator of the soil;—a vocation far more independent, far more sure of success, far more promotive of quiet and happiness, and far better calculated to effect in us moral and religious improvement, than any other. North Carolina, however, is not behind any other State in the Union, in the advantages she offers to skilled mechanics, manufacturers and miners. The raw material for the construction of all kinds of buildings, mechanism, machinery and for every species of manufacture and for mining, is found in North Carolina in the greatest profusion. But it is *agriculture*—the cultivation of the soil, as the great instrument for the development of the whole State, that we specially need. When our lands are put into the hands of strong, industrious and skillful farmers, then every other species of progress and improvement will speedily follow.

In the North-west, though much of the lands are immensely rich and productive when brought into cultivation, yet the agriculturalist in that region experiences a great draw-back in the small variety of articles produced upon those lands. Wheat, Indian corn, (suited to stock-raising, but inferior for bread to the corn raised in this State,) oats, rye, barley, buckwheat, beans, cabbage, Irish potatoes, hemp, apples and some other inferior fruits, the grasses and a few other articles, constitute the sum of the products of those States. Under skillful cultivation, these articles are raised in great abundance.

But look at the great variety of products grown in North Carolina: Indian corn of the best kind, cotton, tobacco, wheat of the finest quality, rice, pease, buckwheat, oats, barley, rye, flax, Irish potatoes, sweet potatoes, honey, hops, sorghum, sugar cane, and pea nuts, all which are and can be made in large quantities for exportation. Every species of garden vegetable that can be named grow abundantly: cabbage, green peas, onions, beans, okra, beets of all kinds, turnips of every variety, carrots, parsnips, pepper, tomatoes, cucumbers, celery, squashes, pumpkins, radishes, lettuce, spinach, &c., &c. Melons of all kinds, most delicious. Apples, pears, peaches, and plums of every variety, cherries, apricots, nectarines, pomegranates, quinces, strawberries, raspberries, gooseberries, currants, &c. Besides these, the cranberry grows spontaneously in several sections, and the black-berry, the dew-berry and whortleberry grow wild and in abundance. Wild game is not abundant except in the new settlements, but fish, one of the cheapest articles of food, are found here in great quantities. It is perfectly apparent, therefore to any one, that in no portion of the earth, are the means of living more abundant and within the reach of every one disposed to work than here.

But the intelligent European or Northern farmer will be struck with the meagre product of the lands of North Carolina, in many of the articles above named, as exhibited by the statistics, compared with the character of the soil and the large amount of cultivated lands and population given. I admit the force of this conclusion. Notwithstanding the boast we have made of the fertility and cheapness of our lands, I must confess with shame, that owing to the ignorance, the laziness, and the absence of skill and progress in agriculture in North Carolina, the statistics which have been made of our products, do not give the reader any intelligible idea of the capacity of our lands. The same amount of labor which has been employed, if it had been directed by scientific knowledge, by skillful hands and operated by an improved culture, carefully selected seeds and proper implements, might have doubled, trebled, if not quadrupled our products. But the labor employed has been usually of the rudest and most unskilled kind, badly directed, by rude implements and by a culture, twenty-five or fifty years behind the age. I do not know that there are five thorough, well instructed planters in the State. Were these lands therefore, in the hands of thorough, highly cultivated farmers, the productions of the State would reach almost a fabulous amount.

ADVANTAGE IN TRANSPORTATION.

The heavy and unweildy products of the Northwest and their costly exportation, is a most serious obstacle in the way of success. Frequently before they reach the markets to which they must go, before they can be consumed, the cost of transportation is two or three times the cost of production. What avail therefore, is the immense productiveness of the

Northwestern lands, if the products when sold at home or in a distant market, can scarcely reach the cost of production? To the planter of small means, this is often crushing to him, while the carrier of his products and the merchant who sells them, alone are made rich. In North Carolina it is far different. The planter who is inaccessible to market for his heavy products, only seeks to make enough of them for home consumption, while the greater variety of products in this State, enables him to spend his strength upon lighter and more profitable marketable articles. But in the greater portion of this State, our navigable streams and Rail Roads, with cheap transportation, put our planters in constant competition with the planters of the Northwest in the production of heavy articles, while it gives them a monopoly in the production of our greater varieties and the lighter articles.

ADVANTAGE OF CLIMATE.

The foregoing observations based as they are upon irrefragable facts, are sufficient to satisfy the most incredulous, of the superiority of North Carolina over the Northwest to the new settler and emigrant. But in what I shall say on this head, I will *demonstrate it*, beyond cavil.

In the cold, bleak, inhospitable climate of the Northwest, almost the entire out-door labors of the farm *must* be attended to during the six or seven most pleasant months of the year. Frost, ice and snow render ditching, fencing or plowing, hazardous to health, if not impossible. In North Carolina ditching and draining can usually be performed during all the months but two, and even during these, this labor is interfered with more from wet, than from cold. Fencing can be done at all seasons, so can the collection of muck and other substances for manure. Plowing can be done at almost any season, the cold and wet of winter interfering with this labor, but little less than the drought of summer. The labors of the farm either in or out of doors, are scarcely ever suspended, more than two or three days at a time.

In the Northwest, I learn, that they never think of a succession of two or three crops of the same kind in a season. In North Carolina this is common. Red clover here may be mowed three times in a season, so of timothy and lucerne. Hay may be mowed twice. Corn or wheat or rye or any of the cereals, or cotton, or flax, cannot be produced twice in a year from the same land, but I have known a good crop of corn, or sweet potatoes or pease, grown from the same land after wheat or oats had been taken off.

The different varieties of apples are produced and ripen in all the months from May to November. So of peaches from

June to October. Strawberries can be produced every month but one or two. Irish potatoes may be seeded during winter and spring, so as to produce new crops from May to November. Sweet potatoes may be seeded from the last of April to July. Our sweet potatoe planters in the Eastern part of the State, commence eating them the last of August and continue, when they are well kept, until first of May. Onions may be seeded in September or later for next crop and may be used in May and June. The heat of July and August prevents the growth of onions; or rather when planted or sown, whether full grown or not, the heat and drought of July and August either stop their growth or ripen them. Onions, turnips, beets, parsnips, sown in September or October, may remain in the soil all winter; so of cabbage, kale and lettuce.

Green peas, onions, Irish potatoes, radishes, beets, cabbage, &c., in the Eastern and middle sections of the State, as well as our fruits, are ready for market in Baltimore, Philadelphia or New York, a week earlier than in Virginia, two weeks earlier than in Maryland, three weeks earlier than in New Jersey and Pennsylvania. Our truck farmers are now supplying those markets largely, transportation being very low, in the early season, and are doing well. Moreover, in this land of flowers, honey may be made in abundance, some bee-raisers taking honey from each swarm two or three times a year, leaving enough for the subsistence of this busy insect during winter.

Hop-raising.—In every portion of North Carolina, hops may be raised in great profusion. The Eastern and middle lands of the State are peculiarly adapted, both in climate and soil to the production of the hop in great perfection. It is almost perennial, the roots when once set, yield their annual fruit without replanting, at least, until age or sterility of soil render them unproductive. This is becoming a most important article of culture, and I judge no country is better adapted to the production of hops, than North Carolina.

By proper management, fruits and vegetables of different kinds may be so produced, as to give the planter through the entire year a sufficient supply. Our field productions may be increased beyond computation. There are other sources of employment, also, such as fishing, lumber getting, turpentine and tar making, mining, manufacturing, mechanism and trade. These open a field in North Carolina, which must at a future day furnish the means of subsistence, of comfort, and luxury, for millions of beings, hitherto not contemplated.

With the means of living so abundant, so various, and so cheap, with a climate unsurpassed in salubrity and healthfulness, with a native population inferior to none in the higher and better elements of manhood, and with facilities of the best kind for education and improvement, what country can be more desirable than this, for the Northern settler or foreign emigrant?

In the early days of the settlement of this State, a Swiss colony settled on Neuse and Trent rivers. Some of their descendants are still in that section. The Scotch peopled the Cape Fear Valley with an industrious and hardy population, and the Dutch and Germans peopled our Piedmont country. The descendants of all these are among our best population. Recently, Switzerland, has made the first contribution to our new emigration. I am assured upon good authority that both, the Swiss employees and their employers, are highly pleased—the Swiss with the country, their labors and their fare, and their employers consider them superior to any laborers they have had. I hope they will be soon followed by others, and that Scotland, Holland and Germany, as well as England, Northern Italy and others, and our own Northern and Eastern States, will second the movement.

Wishing you the success in your enterprise which your efforts and aims richly merit, I subscribe myself,

Very respectfully, yours,

WM. E. PELL.

The following able letter is from the pen of Hon. Thos. L. Clingman, late a United States Senator from North Carolina, a gentleman of large observation and experience upon the subject upon which he writes, and one whose name is a household word in Western North Carolina:

RALEIGH, N. C., *April* 7, 1869.

To the North Carolina Land Company:

In compliance with your request, I proceed to give you a concise statement in relation to the western part of our State. As I understand that you will be furnished with articles, by several gentlemen, describing other sections, I will confine my remarks to the western portion exclusively, viz: that elevated table land extending from the Blue Ridge to the Tennessee State line. Almost all of it was embraced in the Congressional District which I represented for more than a dozen years, and even after I became a Senator, I was frequently passing over it. In fact, I have ascended almost all the principal mountains, and, for the purpose of observing the geological and mineralogical features, visited most of its valleys. Its length, extending as it does, from Virginia to Georgia, is not less than two hundred and fifty miles, while its breadth varies from thirty to sixty miles, averaging probably fifty or thereabouts.

It has along its eastern border the Blue Ridge, by which name in North Carolina, is designated the mountain chain that divides the waters falling into the Atlantic from those of the Mississippi valley. Its western boundary is the great ledge of mountains called in different portions of its course Smoky, Iron, Uncha, &c. Though this range is cut through by the streams running to the west, yet it not only has many points higher than any along the Blue Ridge, but its general elevation and mass are greater. There are also a number of cross chains of mountains, the most elevated of which are the Black and Balsam ranges. There are many points exceeding six thousand feet in altitude above the sea, while the lower valleys or beds of the principal streams in the central parts of the plateau, are from two thousand to twenty-five hundred feet above tide water. To give one an idea of the general elevation of the surface, it may be stated that nineteen twentieths of the land will be found between the elevations of eighteen hundred and thirty-five hundred feet above the ocean. It presents, therefore, a delightful summer climate, surpassing, I think, that of any part of Switzerland. The range of the thermometer in summer is from twelve to fifteen degrees (Fahrenheit), below that of the northern cities, rarely going up to eighty-five degrees in the shade at any hour of the warmest days. The air is almost always bracing and exhilerating in a high degree, while no country is more healthy, being not only free from all miasmatic diseases, but favorable even in winter. Having a southern latitude and surrounded on all sides by lower and warmer regions, its winter climate is much milder than that of Northern Virginia or Pennsylvania. It is unusual for the ground to be covered with snow for as much as a week at a time, and the deepest snows commonly disappear in two or three days on all those portions of the ground exposed to the sunshine.

In many instances persons threatened with consumption have found the climate of Buncombe, about Asheville, both in winter and summer very favorable to them. A gentleman who has passed several winters both at Asheville and in Minnesota, says that the climate of the former place is quite as dry as that of the latter and much milder.

The geological formation belongs chiefly to the older series of rocks, and they are generally well disintegrated. There is one remarkable exception, however, in a belt of country extending from the Grandfather mountain southerly, embracing the Linville and Table mountain ridges. This consists mainly of strata of a more recent origin, quartzite, elastic sandstone, (the Itacolumite or diamond bearing rock of Brazil) and certain slates. The soil over this belt is thin, and covered chiefly with white pine, and such shrubs and plants as are found in poor silicious soils. Outside of this comparatively small tract, the soil of the mountain region is remarkable for its fertility. The gneiss, mica, slate, syenite and other hornblendic and ferruginous rocks are well decomposed and have liberated in great abundance fertilizing ingredients. While no part of the section would be termed rocky in comparison with the New England States, yet there is more rock visible on the eastern border of the belt than on the side next to the State of Tennessee. In general the disintegration seems deeper and the soil richer as one approaches the western border. The Yellow and Roan mountains in Mitchell, and the great Smoky mountain in Haywood, Jackson and Macon furnish striking examples of this fact. On these mountains, at an elevation of six thousand feet, a horse will often sink to his fetlocks in a thick black vegetable mould, and the growth, whether timber, grass or weeds, appears to be as luxuriant as in the swamps of the low country. Even the balsam fir tree, which is usually of no great height, attains an altitude of one hundred and fifty feet on the southern side of the great Smoky, a mountain which from its bulk and general altitude, has been designated by Prof. Guyot as "the culminating point of the Alleghanies." The fact that the mountains usually become richer as one ascends them, is doubtless due to the circumstance that being often enveloped by clouds, and kept cool and moist, the vegetable matter slowly decays and is incorporated with the soil, as usually seen on the north or shady side of a hill.

There is no country of equal extent perhaps better timbered than this. Along some of the streams a good deal of white pine and hemlock are to be found, but the forests chiefly consist of hard wood. All the varieties of the oak are abundant and attain a great size. The white oaks in many places are especially large. So are the chesnut, hickory, maple, poplar, or tulip trees, black walnut, locust, and in fact probably every known tree that grows in the middle and northern States of the Union. There are a few treeless tracts on the tops of several of the higher mountains (covered, however, with luxuriant grasses) which the aboriginal inhabitants regarded as the footprints of the evil one as he stepped from mountain to mountain.

Among the most beautiful valleys are the upper French

Broad and Mills river valleys of Henderson and Transylvania. The Swannanoa in Buncombe, the Pigeon river, Richland and Jonathan's creek flat lands in Haywood, and those of the Valley river and Hiwasse in Cherokee and portions of the upper Linville in Mitchell.

While all of the counties contain large bodies of fertile land, perhaps the soil of Yancy and Mitchell is most generally rich, though the lands are more commonly hilly or rolling than they are in several of the other counties. For its valleys and its fertile mountains combined, none of the counties perhaps surpass Haywood.

There are few of the lands of this whole region too steep for cultivation. They produce good crops of Indian corn, wheat, oats and rye. In contests for prizes in agricultural fairs in Buncombe, from one hundred to one hundred and fifty bushels of the former grain have been produced. The Irish potato and the turnip will probably do as well as in any country whatever, and no region surpasses it for grasses Timothy and orchard grass perhaps do best, but clover, red top, and blue grass thrive well. This region seems to surpass all others for the production of the apple both as to size and flavor. Peach trees do well and bear abundantly of fine sized fruit, but they rather resemble such as are grown in New Jersey for example, and are inferior in flavor to those that are produced east of the mountains in this State. The same may be said of melons. The grape is thrifty and grows abundantly. Besides the Catawba, a native of Buncombe, there are many other native varieties some of which are of good size and delicious flavor. As these different kinds do not ripen simultaneously, it would be easy to make such selections for cultivation as to lengthen the period of the vintage and thus increase its product.

All kinds of live stock can be raised with facility. Sheep in flocks of fifty or sixty browse all the winter in good condition. I never saw larger sheep anywhere than some I observed in the Hamburg valley of Jackson county, the owner of which told me that he had not for twelve years past fed his sheep beyond giving them salt to prevent their straying away. He said that he had on his first settling there, tried feeding them in the winter, but observed that this made them lazy, and therefore he had abandoned the practice. The sixty, I saw were quite as large as any of the sheep I observed once in Regent's Park, London, which were said to be the property of Prince Albert.

Horses and horned cattle are usually driven out into the mountains about the first of April and are brought back in November. Within six weeks after they have thus been "put into the range" they become exceedingly fat and sleek. There are, however, on the tops and along the sides of the higher mountains, evergreen or winter grasses on which horses and the horned cattle live well through the entire winter. Such animals are often foaled and reared there until fit for market, without ever seeing a cultivated plantation.

Very little has yet been done with the minerals of this region. There are narrow belts of limestone and marble which are sufficient for the wants of the inhabitants. Iron ores exist in great abundance in many places. The magnetite is found in quantity at many points, and where it is being worked at Cranberry Forge in Mitchell, it yields an iron equal to the best Swede. There is in Cherokee county a vein of hematite which runs by the side of a belt of marble for forty miles, and is in many places from fifty to one hundred feet thick. It is easily worked and affords a good iron. Copper ores are found in many of the counties, and where the veins have been cut in Jackson county, they are large and very promising. Gold has been profitably mined in Cherokee, Macon and Jackson, and lead, silver and zinc are found at certain points. After the completion of the railroads now in process of construction, the chrome ores and barytes may acquire value.

No country is better supplied with water power than this. The streams attain a sufficient size in the higher valleys, and before they escape into the State of Tennessee they have a descent of one thousand feet. The French Broad at Asheville is larger than the Merrimac at Lowel, and falls six hundred feet in the distance of thirty odd miles, and will soon have a railroad along its banks. Every neighborhood has its waterfalls sufficient for all practical purposes.

The prices of land throughout this entire section are very moderate compared with those of similar lands in the northern States, while the population though sparse is quiet, orderly and moral. The negroes, not constituting one-tenth of the entire population, are scarcely an appreciable element. Emigrants with little capital can easily obtain the necessaries of life, and may at once commence the business of stock raising, and cheese, butter and wool, and such agricultural productions as will best bear transportation. Manufacturing and mining operations will soon follow these branches of industry. I have no doubt, if the people of the Northern States knew this region as I do, they would move down in large bodies immediately to take possession of it. The pleasant climate, good soil and beautiful scenery make it one of the most attractive regions in the world. The wealthy citizen will find the greatest inducements to place there his charming Villa, while to the industrious it will afford a comfortable home.

Very Respectfully, &c.,
T. L. CLINGMAN.

For the following interesting letter, the Company are indebted to Hon. Jonathan Worth, late Governor of North Carolina, a gentleman of unquestional integrity and intelligence, and an experienced lawyer and planter.

RALEIGH, APRIL 9th, 1869.

To the North Carolina Land Company:

In response to your invitation that I contribute something for your forthcoming publication, to present to immigrants authentic facts as to the resources of the State and the advantages she offers to those looking out for a settled home; I infer that other contributors will have gone fully into the subject, and I will therefore, confine my brief communication chiefly to the middle or hilly portion of the State, in which I have lived from childhood and with which I am most familiar.

This State extends from the Atlantic, west of the Alleghany mountains, being about five hundred miles long and of the average width of about one hundred and twenty miles. For about one hundred and fifty miles west of the sea coast, the country is generally level. On the water courses and adjacent to Albemarle and Pamlico Sounds, the land is exceedingly fertile, the rest abounding in pitch, pine and sandy lands. Much of this section is underlaid with marl. The piney lands are peculiarly adapted to the Scuppernong grape vine and may be purchased at a low price—say from $1.00 to $2.00 per acre. It produces the most abundant yield of pea nuts, pease and sweet potatoes. Skillful agriculture brings a rich reward to the farmer, and the fisheries and forests give lucrative employment to many of the inhabitants. This section has yielded more than 100,000 bales of cotton this year. Most of it is convenient to navigable waters. The products of the pine, lumber, tar and turpentine, constitute a large part of the exports of the State.

The middle portion of the State, extending west from this belt some two hundred miles to the foot of the mountains, is adapted to the growth of the cereals and tobacco. This whole region, as well as all the State lying west, to the Tennessee line, abounds in streams suitable for running mills or any other manufactories. In this middle region are many excellent flouring mills, and factories for spinning and weaving cotton and wool and making roll and hammered bar iron: there are many iron mines worked and many others not worked—the iron of excellent quality—also lime and coal, in abundance; but hitherto want of cheap transportation, has prevented large operations in iron, coal and lime. In many of the counties in the middle part of the State, are rich mines of gold, silver and copper. Some of these mines in Mecklenburg, Cabarrus, Rowan, Davidson, Randolph, Guilford and other central counties, have been worked with great success. Copper ores also abound in many of these counties and also in Chatham. In the last mentioned county, I learn that a copper mine of extraordinary richness has very recently been opened and is now being worked. In Randolph two gold mines have recently been opened and much rich ores taken out. The proprietors are about putting up machinery and extricating the gold. Much of this ore is, as I learn from a reliable source, extremely rich. In Randolph county there are five mills in full operation by a superior water power, spinning and weaving cotton. They employ many poor families, at renumerating wages, giving employment only to persons of good moral character. All of these middle counties produce in abundance, when well tilled, wheat, corn, rye, oats, tobacco and the best meadow grasses: and some of the more southern of them—Richmond, Montgomery, Anson, Cabarrus, Mecklenburg and some others produce much cotton. On most of this central part of the State are excellent orchards of peach, pear, apple and other fruit trees. With a pleasant and healthy climate and cheap lands, this region is truly inviting to the immigrant.

The western or mountainous division of the State, embracing about one third of its area, is probably equal to any in like extent of the earth's surface, for the growth of Irish potatoes, clover, oats, rye, blue grass, and other grasses suitable for the making of hay, pasturage, the raising of stock and the productions of the dairy. It has iron ore in abundance, any amount of water power which can be made available for propelling machinery at trifling expense, marble, copper ores, lime, &c.; and owing to its bracing atmosphere, pure cool water, and the abundance of its production of articles of healthful subsistence, has a remarkably vigorous population, almost all of the Anglo Saxon race. In many of the counties of the eastern division of the State negroes abound: in the middle counties are many negroes: in the western counties nearly the whole population is white.

Want of navigable water courses and railroads has retarded the settlement of the western division of the State, in all other respects so attractive. We have a railroad from Morehead City on the Atlantic, *via* Newbern, Goldsboro, Raleigh, Salisbury and Charlotte, from which last place there is railroad communication with Charleston, Savannah and the Mississippi. We have also a railroad from Wilmington *via* Goldsboro to Weldon, whence there is railroad communication to Petersburg and Portsmouth, in Va.—also a railroad from Greensboro' to Danville, Va. We have also a railroad from Raleigh to Weldon—and a branch of the North Carolina Road, completed from Salisbury to Morganton, and the necessary appropriations made and the work in progress for connecting this branch with the Tennessee Railroads. We have also a railroad from Wilmington to the South Carolina railroad connecting with Charleston—also the Wilmington, Charlotte and Rutherford Railroad completed to Rockingham, and the further construction in progress with means provided, supposed to be adequate to its completion. We have also a railroad from Fayetteville, the head of steam boat navigation on the Cape Fear river to the Coal Fields on Deep river, shortly to be extended to some point on the North Carolina Railroad. The Legislature has appropriated $500,000 to complete this extension. The State, by recent legislation, has provided for a large expansion of our works of Internal Improvement.

It may be asked why is a State, presenting such attractions to the immigrant, so sparsely settled? I think the chief cause of the sparse settlement is, that prior to our impoverishment by the late war, and the emancipation of our slaves, not much of our good lands were in market, and no pains was taken to invite immigration.

I believe there is no more law abiding people in America, than the population of North Carolina, and I believe every really brave man, who belonged to the United States army and faced our soldiers as foemen worthy of his steel, and who has settled among us since the war, to follow any other occupation save partizan politics, will say he has no occasion to complain of his reception, socially or otherwise.

During my administration as Governor, beginning in December 1865, to the time of my removal in July 1868, not a single instance occurred in the State, so far as I know, where a Sheriff had to call on his posse, much less for military aid, to enable him to execute any process—

and I believe North Carolina, as to statistics of crime since the war, may safely challenge comparison with any State in the Union.

We hope the time has come when worthy immigrants from Europe, or from any of the States lately waging war against us, will settle among us, bringing with them their capital, or their strong arms, to aid in developing our resources. All such may be assured of a cordial reception.

JONATHAN WORTH.

The following letter from the Hon. D. M. Barringer, late U. S. Minister to Spain, will be read with great interest. It presents very lucidly and ably the points touched upon.

RALEIGH, N. C. *April 10th*, 1869.

To the President and Directors of the North Carolina Land Company:

GENTLEMEN:—The different parts of North Carolina are so dissimilar in climate, soil and geological organizations, that it is impossible, in a brief yet comprehensive manner, to describe its territory, productions and general topography. This want of uniformity, is, perhaps, more characteristic of this than of any other State in the Union. Amid the mountains of our Western border, some of whose peaks are the most elevated East of the "Rocky Mountains," one is continually reminded of the soil and climate of Switzerland and the Upper Rhine, except in the presence of perpetual snow in certain portions of the Alps. In the Eastern part of our State, we have a country which resembles Southern Italy in a remarkable degree, in most of its natural characteristics, and with a soil very much like that of Holland.

And, then again, there is a larger and more central section of the State, which may be compared, and, when more highly cultivated, will present a striking resemblance to large portions of Northern Italy and Southern France.

It is this diversity in the physical appearance and condition of North Carolina, which has given to the world and even to the people of the United States, such contradictory impressions of our soil, climate and productions, and marred even our school books with gross errors, and the most meagre and imperfect information.

A traveller passing along the sea coast would imagine it a barren waste, almost uninhabitable, till informed that it abounded in the most valuable timber—in the best grasses, figs and other fruits, and fish and oysters—and that the Delta of the Nile is not richer than portions of it can be made by proper drainage and cultivation.

Another stranger going through the region of our long-leaf pine, before its agricultural capacities were so fully developed as at present, (and this, in the early period of our history, was the chief line of land-communication between the North and the South,) would realize the impression obtained from the stereotyped blunder of the geographies, even still extensively circulated and believed, that the "staple productions of North Carolina are *tar, pitch and turpentine, and a few naval stores.*"

While another travelling only in the mountains, would suppose that, were it not for the stories he might hear of the wolf, the bear and other wild animals, North Carolina would be a great country for *cattle* and the *dairy* and for *sheep-husbandry* and the like.

And yet another traveller through the middle and central portions of our State, in mid-summer would exclaim, what a fine country this could be made under an improved system of agriculture, for all the productions of the temperate zone, with wine and fruits of all kinds, minerals the most precious and various, and with water power sufficient to run all the factories in the United States!

The truth is, that such is the great *diversity* of our climate and soil—extending from 34 to 36½ North latitude and from the Atlantic to and beyond the Alleghanies, there is scarcely any thing grown from the earth, that could not be successfully produced within our borders under skilful culture and a good system of agriculture.

Being informed by your President that your Company has already been furnished with sketches of the Eastern and Western portions of the State, I will confine any additional observations to a brief description of the resources and the geographical and climatic character of the great *middle or central belt*, lying between the alluvial and pine regions of the East, and the base of the mountain ranges of the West, and extending from the line of Virginia on the North, in a South-westerly direction to that of South Carolina on the South. This portion of the State embraces some thirty-five counties, with an average, in size, of about 600 square miles each, being altogether a little more than one-third of the entire State.

Physical Geography. The surface of this section is generally undulating—with hill and valley and much first and second bottom-land, on the many streams which intersect it in all directions. It is some times called the "hill country" of the State, as contra-distinguished from the low lands of the East and the mountains of the West. There are but few mountains in this part of the State, the principal of which are in Randolph, Cleveland, Lincoln and the "Pilot" in Surry. The foundation or subsoil in the up-land, is generally clay, and the land, in general, is susceptible of the highest cultivation; and, perhaps, no soil in the United States exceeds, in natural fertility, the valleys of the Roanoke, the Taw or Tar, the Neuse, the Cape Fear, and especially those of the Yadkin and Catawba rivers, which traverse the beautiful Piedmont region of the State. These rivers, flowing generally in a South-eastern and Southerly direction, with their many tributaries extending even to the borders of Virginia, effect the drainage of this important section of the State, and furnish every facility for the most extensive water power which may ever be needed by the densest population. These streams have, in general, a rapid flow in their upper courses, while in their lower waters, they are capable of steam boat and light-craft navigation to within short distances of the Eastern and Southern borders of the section I am now attempting to describe, while several of them are capable of *slack-water* navigation, within its actual limits

Climate. This portion of the State is as healthy as any other of equal extent *any where*, and there is no general cause of malaria. There is no need of acclimation, and people from any part of the world can reside here with as little danger from the climate as any where else in the same area of territory.

Products. All the cereals for the support of man or beast, are produced in this part of North Carolina. Indian corn, oats, rye, barley, and especially wheat, of a very fine quality, are made in every locality. While in the more Northern counties, tobacco of a very superior quality is grown in large quantities; and in the Eastern and Southern counties, especially in the tier on the borders of South Carolina, cotton is cultivated with much success and of excellent grade, with little danger from the causes which some times produce a failure of the crop in the more Southern States. Charlotte, Fayetteville, Raleigh, Goldsboro' and Wilmington, are the market centres of a considerable and increasing trade in this great staple of the South.

Cattle and stock of all kinds may be raised in all-sufficient quantities for a very dense population and much for export.

Grasses, of various sorts, are grown to some extent, and this most important culture may be, and with our improving agriculture will be, indefinitely extended in all this region of the State.

The Grape is indigenous in every county, and a great variety of this most valuable vine, is to be found in North Carolina. It is difficult, and not now necessary, to refer to them in detail. But there is one, a native and peculiar, originally, to this State and grows here better than in any other State, which ought, and will some day attract capital and skill in its manufacture of wine, to a degree not surpassed, even, in the most celebrated wine districts of Europe. I refer to the famous "Scuppernong," in its several varieties. Though found, to some extent and yielding fruit in the more eastern and southern counties of the District I am describing, it is chiefly confined and of most luxuriant growth and yield in the eastern counties nearer the coast. It is a marvel in the history of the grape, and its size and rich and most abundant fruit, would astonish the vine-growers of Europe. It needs no pruning, like other vines, and wants only space and light and heat from the sun. The arbor from a single vine often covers a quarter of an acre of ground, and its age will reach beyond the memory of man. Its fruit contains all the elements of, as good a wine, as may be found any where in the world. All we want is a real knowledge of its intrinsic value and skill in its manufacture. I once heard that eminent chemist and analizer, Dr. Warren, of Boston, say, in public, before the "American Association for the advancement of Science," that the time would come when the "Scuppernong" grape, under proper management and skilful manipulation, would make as good a wine as the celebrated "Tokay" of Hungary, and very much like it.

The manufacture of this grape into wine is yet in its infancy, and such is the fondness for it, as a beverage, or from some other cause, no one has ever yet, kept it long enough to furnish a true test of its value and ascertain the effects of *age* and other conditions upon its character and inherent qualities.

Fine grapes may be successfully cultivated and good wine made, by proper care and skill, in almost any part of North Carolina. The late Dr. Emmons, our State Geologist, a man remarkable for his knowledge and science, as well as the truthfulness and modesty of his character, once gave me a sample of wine, made from the wild grape from the lower Cape Fear, which had the genuine characteristics of a good Burgundy and very much resembled the famous "Valde-penas" of Spain.

A residence of several years and extensive travel in Europe enable me to say that, in my opinion, the soil and climate of this State, are peculiarly adapted to the successful cultivation of the grape and the manufacture of wine. And what a blessing they would bring to the morals and happiness, besides adding untold millions to the material wealth, of our people! What we chiefly want in this respect, is an exact knowledge of the identical vine suited to each locality, and then a concentration of our efforts in this direction to its special culture.

The grape vine is wonderfully local in its attachments. All Europe has acted upon this truth—and it will be so here in process of time and experience, and when repeated failures shall have demonstrated its wisdom and the disastrous fallacy of a contrary course. We are trying to cultivate too many varieties, and succeed thoroughly in none. The "Scuppernong" prospers in spite of our neglect, and almost defies our inattention and unskilfulness.

The true and world-renowned "Xeres," or "sherry," as we call it, the "Sherrish-Filistin" of the *Moors*, and the "sherris" of our English "Falstaff," is only made from the grape which is exclusively grown in a small district in the South of Spain, not larger than one of our largest counties. And although millions of gallons of "sherry" so-called, as well as various other adulterated and false wines are made to order at "Cette" in France and many other parts of the world, not excepting our own young America, the genuine brand of the real "sherry" can only be obtained, originally, in the peculiar locality in Spain, where the grape from which it is made, is specially grown under its best native influences; and the real article is manufactured in the *most skilful* manner. So of the genuine "Madeira" and various wines of Germany and France. But excuse this divergence of an enthusiast, perhaps, in behalf of an interest which is destined to become one of the greatest value, in many respects, to the whole Southern portion of the United States, and especially to the State of North Carolina.

Other Fruits. In this portion of the State, fruits of all kinds may be grown to great advantage—both those which spring from the ground, as melons and the like, and all kinds of vegetables, as well as the apple, the pear, the quince, the plum, cherry and other fruits, and especially the *peach*, which comes early and attains much size and perfection in quality, and is very rarely affected by the frost. It is believed that a proper cultivation of this delicious fruit could be made the source of much profit to our people; and the facilities of transportation enable it to reach an early market in the great cities of the North and East.

TIMBER of all kinds, abounds in extensive forests which still exist in their primeval condition, but especially the "Oak," in all its varieties. This central belt may indeed be properly designated as the "Oak" region of the State. For all the purposes of house-building and fencing, wooden-ware and other manufactures, there is every abundance—while on the upper Cape Fear as on the lower, and other localities in the East, there is much suited to the purposes of naval stores and architecture.

MINERALS, of great variety and value, are found in this section of North Carolina. In the counties of Rockingham, Stokes and Chatham, bituminous coal-beds of considerable extent, exist, and only need the facilities which are now being provided for a greatly enlarged development. The coal-beds in Chatham, especially, are very extensive and valuable, and of good quality; and near them, are iron mines of great but undeveloped value, especially the "Black-band" iron, nearly resembling that of Scotland. The "Deep River" mines in this county, have attracted much inquiry and consideration, but owing to various causes, chiefly the lack of easy access and transportation, have not been wrought to any great extent. This want is now being supplied by the completion of the Chatham Rail Road at an early day, which will open communication with other Roads at Raleigh, and thence to the Ocean by the harbors of Norfolk and Beaufort and ports of Wilmington and New Berne.

Deposits of iron are found in many counties in this middle and central district, and of most excellent quality, particularly in the counties of Lincoln, Gaston, Catawba, Stokes, Surry, Randolph and Chatham. In the first named counties they have been worked with success and profit, though in a rude and unskilful manner, from the time of our Revolutionary war. Copper is found in many localities, but chiefly in the counties of Guilford, Davidson, Randolph, Cabarrus, and Mecklenburg. Lead in different places, especially in Davidson, whence, in our recent civil war, a very considerable quantity was obtained for the use of the "Confederate States." Silver and zinc have been discovered and extracted at the same mine, and in other places, but in small quantities. A great many minerals of use in the arts and manufactures, are to be found in different parts of this district of the State, especially *barytes*. But the chief and most valuable of all the metals found in this section is *gold*. It may, indeed, be justly designated as the *auriferous* division of the State, as this precious metal, in more or less quantities, is obtained in nearly all its counties, throughout this whole geological conformation running from North-east to South-west through its entire breadth, and being a part, and the richest part, in this respect, of the same conformation which runs parallel with the whole Alleghany range from the North-east to the South-west of the United States. Gold was here first found early in this century, in the county of Cabarrus, where one piece of twenty-eight pounds, avoirdupois, and many nuggets of less size have been discovered.

From North Carolina, and chiefly from this portion of the State, there have been deposited at the mints for coinage, from *nine* to *ten* millions of dollars worth, since the first discovery of gold in this State: and as the gold found here is in much demand because of its great fineness and malleability, it is supposed, with reason, that nearly an equal amount from the same source, has been consumed in the arts and manufactures. It has been found, principally, in the following counties, in the order in which they are mentioned, viz: Cabarrus, Mecklenburg, Union, Rowan, Stanly, Montgomery, Moore, Davidson, Guilford, Rutherford, Burke, Lincoln, Gaston, Catawba and Franklin. With improved machinery and additional capital, now so much needed, there is every reason to believe that this great interest, in particular, and mining in general, will rapidly and greatly revive and become a source of immense wealth.

Inter-communication. Besides the ordinary highways and public roads, there are Rail Roads already in operation, and others in process of construction, and others also projected, which traverse almost every part of this central division of the State.

The North Carolina Rail Road, from Goldsboro to Charlotte, 223 miles, passing by Raleigh, the capital of the State, runs through this entire section.

The Raleigh & Gaston Rail Road from Raleigh to Weldon, connecting these with three other lines, is 98 miles long, and is the thoroughfare from this State to the great port of Norfolk on the Atlantic Ocean.

The Western Rail Road from Fayetteville on the Cape Fear to Chatham county, and to be continued still farther West. The Rail Road from Wilmington to Weldon, 170 miles.

The Wilmington, Charlotte & Rutherford Rail Road, a large portion of which is completed along the tier of counties on the South Carolina border, to the base of the mountains, and to be extended beyond them towards the West.

The Western Rail Road North Carolina from Salisbury, on the North Carolina Rail Road towards, and across the mountains, now finished to Morganton, in Burke county, in their vicinity.

The Rail Road from Charlotte in a Northwesterly direction, now in process of construction, to the Tennessee line.

And the Chatham Rail Road, a most important connection from Raleigh to the Coal and Iron beds in Chatham county, nearly completed for that distance, and to be continued in a Southwestern direction to and through South Carolina to Columbia, the capital of that State, where it will connect with other great lines to the South and Southwest, &c. Other important roads are projected, and will certainly be completed, affording to this section of the State every facility which may be needed for travel and transportation.

The chief *export markets* for this region are Wilmington, New Bern and Beaufort, in N C., Petersburg, in Va., Charleston, in South Carolina, and, above all, Norfolk, in Va., the best port of the South, and destined soon to become its chief mart and point of export for its great staples. It is one of the best, safest, and largest harbors in the Union, with easy entrance to the Ocean, never ice bound, landlocked, and with a commanding and central position, in the middle of the Atlantic Coast, and having connection with all the great lines of communication in the country. It is near the border of North Carolina, and receives a very large portion of our trade and productions.

Cities and Towns. There are no large cities in North Carolina. The chief interior ones are Raleigh, Charlotte, Salisbury, Greensboro, Fayetteville, Goldsboro, &c., &c., and on the coast those already mentioned. Our population is nearly altogether rural and agricultural. The section under consideration is the most prosperous and wealthy in the State. But compared with the density of population in European countries, and even our own at the North and West, it is sparsely inhabited, though capable of sustaining, in comfort and prosperity, a population as great per square mile as that of Germany or France.

We are now greatly in need of men and money—but especially the former, to till our unoccupied lands and engage in the useful arts. Our labor is greatly demoralized and our whole property depreciated and nearly lost to us by the results of the recent civil war. Our chief want now is a large immigration of men of industry and skill and enterprize, to build up our waste places and help us to restore our lost prosperity. A rich field invites the immigrant who may come from any part of the world, in good faith, to live and remain among us, and make our destiny in the future his own. A social, moral, religious and cultivated people will bid him a hearty welcome. A large portion of the inhabitants now here, are the descendants of those who came to our shores from the North of Ireland, and all the countries of the upper Rhine in Germany and Switzerland. Now is the time to come and buy or rent lands and establish homes among us.

With extensive and personal knowledge of countries, both in Europe and America, I venture to say that, at the present time, there are few better regions for good men to come to, from the redundant populations of any part of the world, than our own Southern land, and especially the good old State of North Carolina.

Asking your indulgence for any omissions or faults in this imperfect compliance with your request, and wishing your Company every success in their very useful enterprize,

I am, gentlemen, very truly and
respectfully, your obedient servant,
D. M. BARRINGER.

The annexed letter from His Excellency, Gov. Holden, present Governor of the State and long the editor of the *Standard*, a leading journal of the State, will be read with interest:

EXECUTIVE OFFICE,
Raleigh, April 13th, 1869.

To the North Carolina Land Company:

GENTLEMEN:—Allow me to express my approval of the object of your Company, and the hope that it may do much good in attracting immigrants and building up the State.

No State on the American continent can present greater inducements to immigrants than North Carolina. The State contains nearly every variety of soil, with a climate of a most salubrious and agreeable nature. Much of the country is still of the untouched original growth, while the most valuable minerals of nearly all kinds abound in every locality, from the beginning of the hill country to the Tennessee line.

The State is now thoroughly reconstructed politically and civilly, and is pushing forward its works of improvement with commendable energy. Large expenditures are being made on this account, thus affording employment to labor and developing our resources. It is expected that the great through line of rail road communication with the Mississippi valley will be completed at an early day, thus connecting the State not only with the trade and travel of that valley, but with the rich regions further west, through which the Pacific Rail Road is located. One of the main branches of this latter work, which is destined to shed the most beneficient results on the whole country, will in all probability, extend through a large portion of North Carolina, from Ducktown, thus pouring the wealth of the West into our own seaports and the port of Norfolk, Virginia.

In addition to these improvements it should be known that the State is making provision for free public schools in every neighborhood. Internal improvements and common schools. which formed the leading policy of the State previously to the late rebellion, will be cherished still more in the future by our whole population.

The laws are every where enforced. Society is tranquil. Every one is free. Consience is unrestrained. There is nothing of an arbitrary character in any of our laws. The country we inhabit is for the most part new, when we consider modern means and appliances for improvement, which have been originated by science and art and sanctioned by practical experience.

Wishing you, gentlemen, very great success in the laudable and useful work in which you are engaged, I have the honor to be,

With great respect,
Your obedient servant
W. W. HOLDEN,
Governor.

To Prof. Kerr, the State Geologist, we are much indebted for the following letter, embodying a large amount of scientific information in regard to the minerals of North Carolina and its adaptation to Agriculture:

GEOLOGICAL OFFICE,
Raleigh, N. C., *April* 15th, 1869.

To the North Carolina Land Company:

According to your request, I have prepared the following abstract of the Geological Reports of North Carolina, showing the mineral and other resources of the State and their distribution. It is, with some additions, the same paper which was published two years ago as an *addendum* to my first Geological Report.

Geographically, North Carolina is situated half way between New York and the Gulf of Mexico, being included between the parallels of 34 degrees and 36 1-2 degrees. It extends from the Atlantic coast five hundred miles westward stretching more than one hundred miles beyond the Blue Ridge mountains, and contains an area of 50,704 square miles, having therefore about the same extent as the State of New York. This territory divides itself naturally into three well marked sections: On the West, the mountainous plateau, having an elvation of 2,500 feet above the sea, and being traversed by several chains of mountains, many of whose peaks attain an elevation of nearly 7,000 feet. On the East lies a low plain, nearly level, partly alluvial and partly sandy, extending about 150 miles from the coast; and between these two spreads the hill country, whose elevation rises gradually from 200 or 300 feet, on the East, to 1200 feet at the base of the mountains.

The eastern section is mostly covered with pines (*Pinus australis and P. tæda*), the middle and western with vast forests of oaks (of many species) interspersed with the poplar, hickory, walnut, maple, &c. Seven large rivers, with their numerous tributaries, traverse the State, furnishing unlimited water power as they flow down from the mountains through the middle section; and as they move with a moderate current, across the champaign country, on the east, into a chain of sounds which skirt the coast, they furnish, with these, an aggregate of 900 miles of inland navigation, which might be doubled by carrying westward the system of slack water improvements already commenced. With these navigable waters is interlaced the railroad sysem of the State, amounting to more than 1000 miles completed, and as much more in progress, which, with about 350 miles of plankroads and turnpikes, bring the sea coast into ready communication with every part of the State.

THE SOIL.

is very various; alluvial and peaty accumulations abound near the coast and along the rivers, while in the middle and western regions the soil is mainly of granitic origin, and represents every grade of sandy or clayey loam of various fertility.

THE CLIMATE.

has also a wide range, being tempered on the seaboard to something like the mildness of that of the Gulf States, while in the mountain region it approaches the rigor of

New York. In the middle section, which constitutes the larger part of the State, and represents the average climate, the mean annual temperature is 60 degrees (Fahrenheit)—the mean Summer temperature 75 degrees, mean Winter 43 degrees, extreme Summer (diurnal) 89 degrees, average maximum 99 degrees, extreme Winter (diurnal) 20 degrees, average absolute minimum 12 degrees. The annual fall of rain is 45 inches. The number of cloudy days in the year is 130; rainy days, 60.

The latitude of the middle of the mountain plateau is about 35½ degrees; and since the average elevation is 2,500 feet, and 500 feet of difference of elevation are about equal, in climatic effect, in the temperate zone, to 1 degree of difference of latitude, the climate will be found to correspond to that of northern Virginia and southern Pennsylvania.

The most elevated portion of it, in Mitchell and Watauga, (above three thousand feet) has the summer temperature of New York seventy-two degrees; and the winter temperature of Washington City, thirty-five degrees; mean annual, fifty-six degrees. The annual rainfall is likewise that of New York, forty-two inches. Snow falls here about as often as in New York, but not more than half as deep. On the lower plateaus, as the French Broad, the elevation of which is a little below two thousand feet, the winter climate is proportionably milder.

THE VEGETABLE PRODUCTIONS.

are numerous. The most important are wheat, corn, oats, rye, potatoes, sweet potatoes, pease, rice, cotton, tobacco, turpentine, grapes and fruits. Wheat and corn are produced with facility and abundance in all parts; rye, oats and potatoes flourish in the middle and western regions; rice, sweet potatoes and pease in the eastern; tobacco in the middle; cotton in the southern counties of the middle, and in the eastern section; turpentine and pine lumber are peculiar to the East. The fruits most extensively and largely cultivated are the apple, peach, pear and cherry, represented by numerous varieties. No part of the continent is better adapted to these than the middle and western regions. The principal grasses are the orchard, herd's, timothy and blue, to which must be added clover and lucerne. All these flourish in the middle and western regions, and some of them grow wild; hence, stock raising is easy and profitable. The stock chiefly raised are horses, mules, cows, sheep and hogs. The grapes usually cultivated, besides foreign varieties, are the Scuppernong, Catawba, Lincoln and Isabella, all natives of the State, the first three being excellent wine

7

grapes. The Scuppernong is peculiar to the eastern section. The following abstract from the United States Census report, for 1860, will best show the productions and capabilities of the State:

Live Stock, - -	3,326,000,	annual product.		
Wheat, - - - -	4,700,000	bushels,	annual	product.
Corn, - - -	30,000,000	"	"	"
Oats, - - - -	2,800,000	"	"	"
Rye, - - -	537,000	"	"	"
Peas, - - - -	1,900,000	"	"	"
Potatoes, - -	830,000	"	"	"
Sweet Potatoes, - -	6,140,000	"	"	"
Cotton, - - -	58,000,000	pounds,	"	"
Tobacco, - - -	32,900,000	"	"	"
Rice, - - -	7,600,000	"	"	"
Wool, - - - -	883,000	"	"	"
Honey, - - -	2,055,000	"	"	"
Turpentine, - -	1,000,000	barrels,	"	"

PRODUCTS OF THE MOUNTAIN REGION.

Timber.—The forests of the mountain plateau are very heavy, and contain an incalculable amount of valuable timber. There are hundreds of square miles of white oak forests, which must become immensely valuable for export at no very distant day. The black locust covers large tracts of territory in many of these counties. This is the most durable timber in our forests, and is so much esteemed for ship building that it is cultivated in the northern States on a large scale, one acre on Long Island, for example, being valued at two to four hundred dollars. Chestnut timber is everywhere. Poplar (tulip tree) is abundant. These two are the largest growth of the mountain forests, sometimes measuring ten to twelve feet in diameter. Not far behind these in size is the black oak (water oak of the mountaineer.) White pine abounds in all the higher plateans, *e g.*, on upper Linville, Elk and New River, (South Fork,) and often reaches a height of one hundred and fifty feet and a diameter four to five feet. Hemlock is also very abundant along the streams in the higher regions, and attains a great size. Among valuable cabinet timbers, mountain birch, (mahogany of the mountaineer,) birds-eye maple, black walnut and cherry are found in great quantities, and of large size. Large fields have been fenced with black walnut in this region. I measured a cherry tree in Elk bottom, which is more than nine feet in girth, and seventy-five feet to the first limb. Such a tree would be worth more than one hundred dollars in New York. There are also extensive forests of sugar maple, from which many thousands of pounds of sugar are manufactured every year, supplying the entire home market in many sections. The linn tree, (*tilia,*) which is abundant in the rich coves, is highly prized by the inhabitants, as furnishing a valuable winter forage for cattle.

Besides timber there are other spontaneous products that are worthy of mention; among which are

Cranberries.—There are hundreds of acres of native cranberry beds on the streams in the higher valleys, from which large quantities of fruit are annually gathered for export. To which may be added

Medicinal herbs.—Of these ginseng is the most important. Several hundred thousand pounds of this article are annually exported, and it is a source of large revenue to the inhabitants. North Carolina and Minnesota are the principal sources of this export, the whole of which goes to China. Wild ginger (*asarum*) is also an article of considerable trade, as well as several kinds of snake root, pink root, puccoon, hellebore, lady's slipper, spikenard, Indian turnip, Indian hemp, and a hundred others. The aggregate amount of money realized annually from the trade in these articles in the mountain section of this State is probably over a quarter of a million.

The principal farm products are corn, wheat, rye, buckwheat, oats, grasses, (chiefly timothy, herd, blue, orchard and clover,) fruits, (especially apples, occasionally peaches, pears and grapes,) potatoes, and root crops.

Corn grows everywhere. On the higher ridges and plateaus (three thousand feet and upwards) the northern varieties are required on account of the shortness of the seasons.

Wheat does well in Buncombe, Madison, Yancey, and in small portions of the other counties.

Rye, buckwheat, oats and the grasses flourish everywhere, but especially in the more elevated regions of Mitchell, Watauga, Ashe, Yancey, &c. I am assured by intelligent farmers in this region that four tons per acre of hay is no uncommon yield. These grasses escape from cultivation and propagate themselves everywhere. I have seen a field near five thousand feet high that was seeded, some twenty years ago, with timothy, and has not been under fence in fifteen years, which has still a good "set" of grass. Oats grown at this place weighed forty-two pounds per bushel.

In the higher parts of the mountains, (above four thousand five hundred feet,) there are three species of perennial winter grass, which send up their new shoots, or stools, in November, and remain green all the year; so that cattle and sheep require little care even in winter, except in case of a deep fall of snow, which does not happen more than once in eight or ten years.

The new Japan clover, as it is called, (*Lespedeza striata,*) has spread over the whole of this region. I have found it in a few cases on the tops of mountains four to five thousand feet high. Such facts as these, taken in connection with the exceeding cheapness of land, and the proximity to the great markets of the country, will surely justify the opinion that the continent does not afford more favorable conditions for profitable cattle farming, wool-growing and cheese making.

The President of the Cheese Makers' Association of New York (Gov. Seymour) stated the other day in an address, that the reason of their ability to compete successfully with the English cheese makers is to be found in the comparative *cheapness of land in* New York. The price of one acre of Governor Seymour's grass land will buy two or three hundred acres in this region.

Cheesemaking has recently been introduced here by a few intelligent and enterprising citizens of Buncombe and will no doubt soon establish itself as a leading industry of the mountain section.

It is inexplicable that no one has undertaken wool-growing on a large scale, as such an enterprise, judiciously conducted, could scarcely fail of success.

Apples.—Fruit growing must also prove very profitable, now that transportation is to be furnished. No part of the continent produces the apple in greater perfection, or with less cost and trouble. There is scarcely a county that has not several *accidental* seedlings of fine quality; and apples are frequently produced of twenty-two to twenty-three ounces weight; (and even much larger figures were reported to me, but as I had no means of verifying the statements, I do not venture to repeat them.)

Potatoes here are remarkably prolific, the yield being sometimes as high as six hundred bushels to the acre, and the quality unsurpassed.

Root Crops are abundant and of the best quality, - a fact worthy of note in connection with the subject of cattle raising.

The climate and agricultural characteristics of the piedmont region are notably different. In these respects it much more nearly resembles the middle section of the State, (the hill country.) Corn and wheat are of course the staple products, and near the mountains, rye, &c. A large part of it is well adapted to the growth of tobacco, a plant not much cultivated here however. Fruits grow well everywhere, but particular localities have special adaptation to the growth of certain species. The apple flourishes especially along the foot of the Blue Ridge. On the Brushy Mountains also, in Wilkes County a fruit is produced of peculiar excellence, Both its orchards and vineyards are famous. Lincoln County originated the grape of that name, (called also the "Hart," "Lenoir" and "Davis" grape,) and Buncombe claims the Catawba. Cherry Mountain in Rutherford is noted for its extensive cherry orchards and the unequalled flavor of the fruit. It also produces a rare quality of wheat. The Japan clover has taken possession of this whole piedmont section within a few years, occupying the road sides, fence corners and old fields, and seems likely to exterminate the pestiferous broom grass. This plant is an annual, of comparatively recent introduction, which seems destined to play an important role in the future agriculture of the State. Notwithstanding the differences of opinion among farmers in the regions which it has invaded, it is unquestionable that it has valuable qualities both for pasturage and as an improver of the soil.

Water power is abundant every where, as will be evident from the topography of the country already given in outline, taken in connection with the annual rainfall of forty-two to forty-four inches. The Catawba and Yadkin descend seven hundred feet in a course of sixty miles across the piedmont section from the base of the Blue Ridge; and the thousand tributaries (many of which are themselves respectable rivers) have a much more rapid descent. Beyond the Blue Ridge the case is still stronger. Here is a score of large rivers which precipitate their vast volumes of water from these elevated plateaus through more than a thousand feet of descent in a course of thirty to forty miles, developing an amount of force which is beyond all estimate. The power developed by the Falls of Niagara is estimated to be thirty times as great as the whole amount of utilized water and steam power of Great Britain. The water power of North Carolina is ample for a continent.

THE MANUFACTURES,

are chiefly of cotton, wool, spirits of turpentine, lumber, iron, paper and leather.

The amount invested in the manufacture of cotton is $2,250,000; lumber, $1,000,000; turpentine, $2,000,000; iron, $500,000; wool, $350,000.

FISHERIES

abound in the sounds and rivers of the eastern counties. The species of fish mostly taken are the herring, shad, blue fish, mullet and rock. The number of barrels annually packed for market is about 100,000 on the waters of Albemarle Sound. Considerable quantities are packed at other points.

MINERALS.

A statement of some general principles, and a few observations on the leading geological features of the country, will make the subject more intelligible. The position, general arrangement and condition of the rocks of a region have always an intimate dependence on its mountain systems. The strike, or direction of out-crop of the strata may generally be predicted as soon as the direction of the dominant mountain range is ascertained. Thus the different beds of rocks on the eastern side of our continent fall into parallelism with the axis of upheaval of the Apalachian system. The general direction of the Blue Ridge, therefore, gives us approximately the geological meridian to which all the rocks of North Carolina must be referred. This direction is nearly north-east and south-west. Every one has noted that the edges of the out-cropping strata, and in general the trap dykes and mineral veins, take this direction predominantly in our latitude. The beds of slate, limestone, gneiss, &c., follow each other in regular succession, all trending away to the north-east. So that in passing from the sea coast to the mountains, we cross successively in our track the upturned edges of the whole series. Thus we have the clue to the distribution and arrangement of the rocks in mass.

In the study of the metaliferous minerals, it is important to bear in mind two leading facts: first that they are found, especially the precious metals, chiefly on the flanks of mountains and in tracks marked by disturbance and upheaval, in the vicinity of trap dykes and other eruptive rocks, and at the intersections of these with slate; and second, that their occurrence is most frequent in the older formations, the Primary and lower Secondary.

The rocks of North Carolina belong to this lowest horizon, being wholly included, with the unimportant exception of the coalfields, in the Primary group. So that we are prepared for the statement that there is hardly to be found a territory of the same extent, with so great a variety of valuable minerals. In the treatment of this subject, it will be sufficiently precise for our purpose to divide the useful minerals into two classes, namely, the metaliferous ores, which occur mostly in veins, as gold, copper, &c., and early minerals and rocks, which are found mostly in beds, as coal, limestone, &c.

Under the first division, occur gold, silver, copper, lead, zinc, iron and tungsten, and here, for convenience, may be added the diamond; and under the second, may be mentioned, as occurring in this State under such circumstances, as render them economically valuable, coal, marl, limestone, marble, architectural granite, sandstone, porphyry, fire-stone, buhrstone, grindstone grit, whetstone slate, roofing-slate, alum and copperas slates, soapstone, serpentine, agalmatolite, fire-clay, graphite, garnet, barytes, manganese, oil slates, and chromate of iron.

COAL.

The second division, being most important, will first claim attention; and first among these coal.

The value of this mineral is too well known to require statement even. The development of all arts and industries is connected with its abundance and cheapness. It is found in two districts in North Carolina, known as the Deep River and Dan River Coalfields. In both, the coal is bituminous, and occupies a narrow tract of country along the course of the rivers from which they respectively take their names.

These beds, therefore, follow in their outcrop the general direction of the rocks of the country. The Dan River bed is distant from market, and has been little explored. There is an outcrop in Rockingham and Stokes counties, one seam being four feet thick. The Deep River bed is better known, and probably more extensive. It is described in detail, in the Geological Reports of Dr. Emmons, for 1852 and 1856, and also by Admiral Wilkes, in his reports to the Secretary of the Navy, in 1859. According to these authorities, this coal is of the best quality, well adapted to the manufacture of iron and gas, and is inexhaustible in quantity. They represent it as extending over an area of more than forty square miles, and containing more than 6,000,000 of tons to each square mile. This bed, therefore, would yield 1,000,000 tons annually, for several hundred years.

OIL.

These North Carolina coalfields are cotemporaneous with those of Virginia, and belong to an age more recent than the Apalachian coal formation, which ranges from Pennsylvania to Alabama. They belong to the later ages of the Secondary.

The bituminous slates associated with the coal are strongly impregnated with organic products. Dr. Emmons says, "From thirty to forty gallons of crude Kerosene oil exist in every ton of these slates. They are from fifty to seventy feet thick, and it is proper to state, that it is a better oil than is furnished from coal." The coal lies in a trough-like depression, which extends from Granville county, in a south west direction, to South Carolina. This tract is occupied, in its whole length, by a heavy bed of sandstones, of the same age with the coal. They are identical in appearance, quality and age, with the brown-stone of Connecticut valley, which is so extensively used as a building stone in New York and elsewhere. These sandstones are also extensively quarried for grindstones, for which they are well adapted.

FIRE-CLAY, &C.

Beds of fire-clay, also, are interstratified with the coal. This mineral is found in various parts of the State, conspicuously in Gaston county. There are five or six parallel belts of sandstone and quartzite, belonging to the older rocks, which traverse the State in the prevailing direction, and in which are found various grades of building-stones, fire-stones and grindstones. According to Dr. Emmons, one of these passes eastward of Raleigh, another a few miles to the westward, and a third crosses the counties of Montgomery, Randolph and Orange. The well known fire stones of Gaston, Lincoln and Catawba, occur in the fourth belt, which crops out along the line of upheaval of King's mountain, Crowder's mountain and Little mountain. This rock in places assumes the character of white granular quartz (saccharoidal quartz of the mineralogist) and attains sufficient purity to be used in the manufacture of glass. Linville mountain, in McDowell county, at the eastern base of the Blue Ridge, is chiefly made up of the same rock. Here is found the flexible sandstone (Itacolumite of the mineralogist) in which the diamond occurs in other parts of the world.

LIMESTONE.

In addition to the four beds of this rock in the western counties, there are two beds east of the Blue Ridge; one is in McDowell county, along the North Fork, the other crosses the State from King's mountain, along through Gaston, Lincoln and Catawba to Stokes. There is also a small bed of marly limestone eight or ten miles in length in the northwestern part of Wake county.

PORCELAIN CLAY, &C.

Agalmatolite constitutes another member of the sandstone group in at least two of the zones, being found in this connection in Montgomery and Chatham, as well as on the Nantehaleh river, and across Cherokee county. This rock is miscalled soapstone, which it resembles in some of its properties and uses.

It is developed here on a large scale, and in no part of the world is found in greater purity or extent. Its uses in the arts are manifold, being substituted for graphite in lubrication, and for soapstone in furnaces, prepared as a cosmetic and a pigment, and manufactured into soap, into ornaments, and the finer kinds of porcelain ware. It has been exported for this latter purpose in large quantities to New York, and to Germany.

GRAPHITE.

Here, also, belong the famous graphite, or plumbago beds of Wake county, being found immediately under the sand stone, or quartzite. It occurs, likewise, in the same connection, in the Catawba belt (in Gaston, Lincoln and Catawba) and scattered through several counties westward. The uses of this mineral are well known and important, the principal of which are for the so-called lead pencils, for crucibles, for paints, for lubrication and for electrotyping, &c. The Wake county mines have been worked to a considerable extent, and will, no doubt, be re-opened. Dr. Emmons and Prof. Olmsted pronounce these the most important beds of this mineral known.

The quartzite in Montgomery, takes the form of a buhrstone, which is supposed to be valuable for the manufacture of mill stones. This mineral is also found near Webster, in Jackson county, and on Nantehaleh river, in Macon.

SOAPSTONE, WHETSTONES, GRINDSTONES, &C.

Soapstone and serpentine of good quality are found in various parts of the State, for example, in Wake, Moore, Orange, Randolph, Mecklenburg and Caldwell, and west of the Blue Ridge, there is a remarkable belt of serpentine and chlorite slates, traversing the State from Clay to Mitchell, which carries a great variety of minerals, interesting to the mineralogist, and one at least that might become valuable economically, viz: The slate formation, which occupies a tract of the State, not less than forty miles in width, west of the coal rocks of Deep river, extends in a north-east direction, from Anson and Union counties on the southern border to the Virginia line. These slates constitute a notable feature in the geology of the State, and, in addition to the interest which attaches to the numerous mines along its north-western border, they contain extensive beds of roofing-slates and turkey hones, (novaculite.) Scythe-stones are also found on the Nantehaleh, of good quality and in great abundance.

The Linville Slates furnish abundant materials for grindstones and whetstones, in the Linville mountains, and for whetstones of very good quality in Adam's Nnob on John's River. On Laurel River in Madison is a peculiar cherty splintered whitish quartz rock which Mr. George Gehagan has manufactured into millstones, which are described as nearly equal in performance to the French buhrstone. One of the best millstone grits in the country is found on McLennon's creek, in Moore county.

ALUM AND COPPERAS.

Alum and copperas slates abound in many parts of the State, and have been extensively brought into requisition during the stress of the late war. The counties of Cleveland and Rutherford alone contain not less than 100 square miles of these rocks, and could easily supply the continent with copperas. This material is derived, by the process of weathering, from the iron pyrites which is disseminated, in great abundance, and in a state of extreme comminution, through the slates, many of which, being feldsphatic, yield also alum.

MINERAL SPRINGS.

The same cause, viz: the abundance and wide diffusion of iron pyrites give rise to so many sulphur, chalybeate and alum springs in this Piedmont country. They abound throughout the region, but the most noted are the Wilson's Springs, (White and Red Sulphur, and Chalybeate) near Shelby in Cleaveland county, McBrier's and Patterson's in the same county, and the Catawba White Sulphur and Chalybeate in the northern part of the county of the same name, and Piedmont Springs in Burke near Table Rock. All these are watering places of some celebrity. Wilson's and the Catawba have been recently improved and furnished in good style. They have the advantage of being located in a very salubrious climate, in view of the mountains, and easily accessible from the Rail Roads. Beyond the Blue Ridge also mineral springs abound. The most notable are the celebrated Warm Springs near Ashville, and the Million Springs at the foot of Craggy Mountain.

MICA.

Large crystals of mica are found in many parts of Yancey and Mitchell; the largest I have seen, however, were obtained in Cleveland near Shelby. When clear and free from flaws, plates four inches by six are worth about one dollar and a half per pound.

BARYTES AND MANGANESE.

Barytes is found in Orange, in the mines of Cabarrus and Mecklenburg, also in Gaston and Madison counties; and manganese in Cabarrus and Gaston as well as in Lincoln, Catawba and Chatham.

MARL.

This valuable material is liberally scattered over most of the seacoast section of the State, and is found in every degree of purity and consolidation, from a mere aggregation of loose shells to the most compact limestone, suitable for building or for burning into lime. The famous Bath stone of London is matched by some of these beds. The marl is generally found near the surface and easily accessible. The importance of these accumulations of mineral manure to the agriculture of the State is not fully appreciated. Our farmers are only beginning to understand the essential part which lime plays in the economy of vegetable growth, and its important relations to exhausted soils.

We pass to the other division of minerals, the metaliferous ores.

To the unpracticed eye, nothing presents a picture of more hopeless disorder and chaos than the rocks, particularly in a region of great disturbance, as in a moutainous country.

Here seems truly "A land of darkness, without any order, and where the light is as darkness." And yet, at the touch of science, order rises out of this confusion, and light spreads over this darkness. In a region of the wildest riot of disorder, dislocation, disturbance and inversion, under the patient and inevitable inductions of geology, the upheaved, overturned, and distorted strata fall into rank and regularity along certain axes and group themselves orderly about certain centres. As the sandstones, limestone, &c., of the previous division were found to acknowledge certain relationships *inter se*, and toward a controlling geological meridian, so it will appear that the metaliferous ores are not scattered at random and as if by chance, (even within the limitations already stated, of a disturbed area and a low geological horizon) but have a subordinate grouping and a palpable arrangement.

IRON.

And first of iron, king of metals; so, because it constitutes the very frame-work, as it were, of our material civilization, without which the whole fabric would vanish like the fabled ship on approaching the magnetic mountain. North Carolina is peculiarly fortunate in the possession of an abundance of iron ore, and so widely distributed and in so immediate juxtaposition with the other materials and means for smelting it, that each section, exeept the seaboard counties, can produce its own supply. These ores occupy chiefly five or six narrow tracts, or districts, which have an obvious relation to the mineral belts already pointed out.

This relation is most obvious and most immediate in the trans-Catawba tract, the ore being found in heavy veins along the out-crop of the sandstone from King's mountain through Gaston, Lincoln and Catawba, to Stokes and Surry. A second belt extends through Montgomery, Randolph and Guilford. A third has its largest development in Chatham in the neighborhood of the coal, at Buckhorn, Lockville, Ore Hill, Egypt, &c., but makes its appearance also in Johnson. These ores are specular, magnetic and hematite.

In the coal-beds themselves, exists an importantdeposit of iron ore interstratified with the coal. West of the Blue Ridge is one of the most valuable accumulations of iron ore to be found in the country. It has been long famous for the fine quality of the metal which it yields. The ore lies at the base of the Yellow mountain in Mitchell county, and is found at several points in a southwest direction in Madison and Haywood. These beds are magnetic, and are well adapted to the manufacture of steel.

Another bed accompanies the limestone of McDowell and

Transylvania; and one of the most important and extensive deposits in the country, crosses the entire breadth of Cherokee. It belongs commonly to the variety of specular or hematite ore. The completion of the Western Rail Road will bring these immense deposits into speedy requisition, and will probably render Cherokee the leading iron county of the State.

The manufacture of iron had attained to considerable importance in the State previously to the late war, during which, of course, this industry received a great impetus. And when our system of Internal Improvements shall have been completed, this will doubtless become one of the most important manufactures in the State.

GOLD.

Gold mining commenced in North Carolina about fifty years ago. The first impulse was given to the business by the accidental discovery of some large nuggets in Cabarrus and Anson counties. Previously to the year 1820, not more than $50,000 had been obtained. In 1863, the aggregate yield was not less than $10,000,900; which would make an average annual yield of $250,000. Here, as elsewhere, the first mining was confined to "surface-diggings." And in 1824, Professor Olmsted, of the University, then State Geologist, expressed doubts about the existence of gold veins in that region.

In California, Australia, along the Andes and the Ural,—every where, in ancient and modern times, these superficial deposits have been the chief source of the precious metal, and have been generally more remunerative than vein-mines. And it is in this datritus of sand, gravel and clay, that nearly all the large masses, or nuggets, of gold have been found.

In North Carolina, however, vein-mining has obtained great prominence; and the larger part of the whole product in this State has been derived from this source. Some single mines in the gold region have yielded from one to two millions. And if these mines have not been uniformly profitable, it is because they have been generally wrought with little science, or economy. *Overman, in his work on Metallurgy, has recorded his conviction that these mines, under proper management, would be more profitable than those of California.*

The vein-gold of this State is usually found in a gangue of quartz, or disseminated in a slaty veinstone; and is commonly associated with iron and copper pyrites. This association almost universally prevails below the water-level. These mines, therefore, are of the same character as those of California and Colorado, and the new methods which have been devised during the last few years, to meet the difficulties of working this class of ores will doubtless be found applicable here.

The gold district proper of North Carolina extends, inclusively, from Guilford, Randolph and Moore counties, West and South-west to the Blue Ridge, and comprises all the interjacent counties, some twenty in number. Outside of this region there are but two gold fields of any note, viz: in Cherokee and Nash.

The Reed mine in Cabarrus county has yielded more than a dozen nuggets, of various weights, from twenty-eight pounds (the largest ever found before the discovery of California) to two or three pounds, making an aggregate of over 120 pounds. These nuggets are found in the detrital accumulations of denuded veins. The most extensive surface diggings, or placer mines, are found in the South mountains, occupying nearly 200 square miles in Burke and the neighboring counties. More than a million of dollars have been obtained from this deposit, and it is by no means exhausted.

There are also placer diggings of considerable extent in the counties of Caldwell, Polk and Nash.

SILVER.

It will be observed that the richest gold mines lie along and near the line of contact of the slates and granite. And it is also along this line that the principal silver mines of this State are found. The most noted of these is at Silver Hill, in Davidson county. The combination of metals here is quite complex,—including, with the silver, gold, lead, copper and zinc. A chain of silver mines runs south-west along the western border of the slates, including the Conrad, the McMakin and the Stewart mines. During the war, the first named of these mines yielded a considerable quantity of lead. It had been previously worked chiefly for silver and gold. The same association of metals occurs in Cherokee.

Two or three silver mines have also been discovered recently in Watauga county, near the Tennessee line.

LEAD AND ZINC.

Lead has not been found in quantities to justify operation elsewhere in the State, although its existence has been ascertained in several localities in the mountain region, as in McDowell and Cherokee. Both the silver and lead of North Carolina are found mostly in combination with sulphur in galena.

Zinc is not known to occur in the State, except in the above named association and localities.

The new process of manufacturing zinc paint has rendered all these zinc-lead mines immensely valuable.

COPPER.

Copper has long been known as an accompaniment of gold in most of the mines of that metal especially in those which occur within the belt of granite bordering the slates on the west. Many of these, which were originally operated as gold mines, were abandoned on account of the increase of copper pyrites with the depth; and it is only within a few years that several of them have been re-opened as copper mines.

The mines of this metal in the gold district above indicated, are found East of the Catawba river, and the most important of these are in the Southern portion of Chatham, in Guilford, Davidson, Rowan, Cabarrus and Mecklenburg, many of which have been recently re-opened. There are also several other mines outside of this district, the principal of which is the Gillis mine in Person.

Beyond the Blue Ridge are two well defined copper districts, in which occur many large veins, which have only been opened at a few points. One of these lies on the head waters of the Tuckasegee in Jackson, extending occasionally across the mountain chains into the neighboring counties of Macon and Haywood. The most noted mines in this region are the Cullowhee, Waryhut and Savannah. The other copper belt is in Ashe and Alleghany counties. The important mines here are the Elk Knob, Ore Knob, Peach Bottom and Gap Creek. In both these trans-montane districts, the veins are developed on a very large scale. They differ from all other copper mines in the State (and so far as I know in the country) in being found in hornblende state.

CHROMIC IRON.

As has been stated, this mineral accompanies the serpentine in the most of its outcrops in the transmontane plateau, e. g., in Yancey, Mitchell and Watauga, as well as in Jackson. It exists in the form of nodules and veins. This mineral yields a very large number of valuable paints.

TUNGSTEN.

Tungsten, a metal which was long merely a chemical curiosity, but has recently assumed a high value, particularly on account of its relation to the manufacture of steel, occurs in Cabarrus.

DIAMONDS.

Several valuable diamonds have been found in the trans-Catawba country, in Lincoln and Rutherford counties.

From this very rapid survey of the minerals of North Carolina, several facts worthy of note are evident: first, that, though widely distributed, they are not scattered at random, but follow a certain order of grouping and association; so that the probability of the occurrence of a given mineral in any particular locality can be approximately ascertained before examination.

Again, it is evident that this State is abundantly supplied with the more important and valuable minerals, those which are essential to the permanent and successful development of our agriculture and manufactures. Among these must be always first named iron, coal and lime. Of the first two it has been seen that there is the greatest profusion. Of lime, however, it may be supposed that there is a deficiency. It is true that we have no such immense territory of limestone as is found in some of the other States; and yet, upon consideration, it will be apparent that nature has provided an abundant store for all possible needs. The tertiary region in the east finds an ample supply for the purposes of agriculture and architecture in its widely diffused beds of marl. And although the farmer of the middle and western sections may not always find an imperative need of this fertilizer, his soils being frequently derived by disintegration from rocks which contain a considerable per centage of lime, yet, since the breadth of the State is traversed at comparatively short intervals by a number of outcrops of limestone, which are crossed almost at right angles by our rivers and many of our rail roads, it is thus brought within convenient reach of almost every neighborhood. Nature has denied us only two of the more important mineral deposits, salt and gypsum, (and they may yet be discovered in the sandstone of the coal.) But of these two there is an unlimited store just across our borders, within easy reach by a short line of railroad, of our net-work of proposed and completed rail roads and of our rivers. Taking, then, in one view, our resources of iron, coal, and lime, of gold and copper, and the great variety of other minerals of subordinate but real and increasing value, it is sufficiently apparent that our State has here the foundation of indefinite wealth and prosperity; and that there is wanting to these ends only a vigorous prosecution of our system of internal improvements on the part of our Legislature, and intelligence, industry and enterprise on that of our citizens.

THE POPULATION

in 1860 was 992,622, of which one third are colored, and 3,298 are of foreign birth. One-tenth of the population live in towns and cities.

LAND.

According to the census of 1860, there were 6,500,000 acres of improved land, being about one fifth of the area of the State. The price at which these lands are held ranges from about 3 dollars to 100 dollars per acre; the average would be about 7 1-2.

The only qualification necessary to enable a foreigner to own land, is taking the oath of allegiance to the State, or becoming a citizen of the United States.

PUBLIC SCHOOLS

were maintained in the State, by the means of the income derived from the Literary Fund, which amounted to two million five hundred thousand dollars in 1860. About half of this fund has been swept away by the war; and the system of District schools which had brought a rudimentary education within the reach of all, free of cost, has been entirely prostrated for the present, but will be revived immediately under laws recently enacted for the purpose.

The State may be reached directly from Europe through either of her ports—Wilmington or Beaufort, (or Norfolk,) from which railroads penetrate every part of the State.

From New York the distance by railroad or steamer is about 20 hours.

The number of newspapers published in the State is about 75; all in the English language.

Yours, truly,

W. C. KERR,
State Geologist.

The following letter addressed to a New Yorker, is from the pen of our venerable and learned friend Rev. Dr. Mason, Rector of Christ's Church, Raleigh, N. C. It will be read with interest:

RALEIGH, N. C. *April* 20, 1869.

MY DEAR FRIEND:—From what you have heard of the climate of North Carolina, and especially of that middle belt in which Raleigh is situated, you think it possible you may forsake the cold regions of New York for the milder winters of this State. You wish me then to tell you, how I like my residence here, what I really think of the climate, especially of Raleigh; what is the character of the country generally; what its agriculture, and what prospect there is of your carrying out successfully your favorite amusement or pursuit, shall I call it, of gardening.

My answer to the first, need not be long. You know I have been here many years, and you have never heard me, I am persuaded, express any intention or desire to remove.

For the healthiness of the country, that must depend on the part of the State in which one resides. The eastern part of the State must be to a greater or less degree subject to intermittent and remittent fever. I do not think however, it can be in this respect much, if at all, worse than the eastern part of Virginia or Maryland; and must be far better than the eastern part of South Carolina, and consequently of Georgia, if there is any foundation for the old woman's impression. When the line was run between North and South Carolina, her house was determined to be in the North instead of the South State. At this she expressed great satisfaction, as she had always heard that South Carolina was a desperate unhealthy place. You know I have lived in various climates. I have been in the West India Islands, at least in one, the most healthy perhaps of them. I have resided in three of the Northern States, as far as New York, but I can certainly say, that I consider the climate of Raleigh much superior to any I have ever been in. The air is dry; there are no swamps or marshes around us; the soil is generally porous; the violence of northeastern storms does not reach us, nor the unwholesome moisture of the South-east; both are tempered before they reach us.

I have known many persons in a population of between five and six thousand, more than eighty; a few, more than ninety years old; and as far as my experience goes, the young are less liable to die here than in any place I have ever lived. What my experience has taught me of Raleigh is true, I believe, of the whole belt of country extending from the Virginia to the South Carolina line in which Raleigh is situated. It is intermediate between the east with its intermittent and remittent fevers, and the west with its more inflammatory disorders. Diseases of both sorts exist among us, but far less frequently than in their native regions, and generally very much modified in violence. We have no endemic diseases and epidemics very seldom occur; I never knew or heard of a genuine case of cholera.

As I know your aversion to musquitoes, I may say for your satisfaction that although they are to be found in Raleigh in some parts of the town, but not in great numbers, in other parts of the town they scarcely show themselves at all; and in any part, they are, compared with eastern musquitoes such insignificant fellows, that were it not for the villainous drone of their hateful bag-pipes you might despise them altogether.

Of the face of the country: North Carolina, you know, may be considered a long parallelogram divided into three distinct regions; the flat country of swamps and marshes and sluggish streams, supposed, I think, by geologists to have been upheaved from the sea, and extending about one hundred miles from the coast. A great part of this region is sandy, and easily worked, is very fertile, abounding, however, in the long-leaved pine, from which turpentine, &c., is obtained, and for which North Carolina is noted. These sandy lands, when improved by manuring and otherwise skillful cultivation, make very good cotton lands.

Two sources of fertility have been resorted to, one mineral and the other vegetable. The eastern region of the State abounds in marl beds, and these are beginning, indeed have been for some time, used very successfully by certain persons in certain districts. The other, and vegetable source of improvement is called the corn or field pea, producing an abundant stalk and foilage, and when sowed in early summer and plowed in when near maturity, supplies, in the Southern States, the place of clover in the Northern States, with a more rapid effect.

The swamp and marsh lands, when cleared and drained, are very fertile. I have heard of some of them producing from eighty to a hundred bushels of corn per acre, and of an hundred dollars an acre being refused for their purchase.

The middle region is the region of wheat and corn, along its northern borders, of tobacco very excellent, and in some counties, cotton. Along the Southern border, besides the first named products of wheat and corn, the chief production is cotton. Some of the counties of this region are quite fertile, some not remarkably so.

The third region, the mountainous and most westerly part of the State, is, I am told, a magnificent region. Of all the mountain country of the United States east of the Rocky mountains, the mountains of N)rth Carolina are the loftiest, and yet they are clothed with verdure from top to bottom. In this part of the State, there is perhaps, as excellent a grazing country as can be found in the United States; may be in any part of the world. The soil, too is a wonderful producer of roots and tuberous plants. I have heard of one thousand bushels of the common potatoe—Irish as we call them to distinguish them from sweet potatoes—being produced on an acre. This may be an exaggeration or myth, but all myths have some reality, all exaggerations have some foundation.

Thus you will see that North Carolina being situated between Virginia and South Carolina, partakes of the agricultural advantages of both. It must be considered as the extreme north of cotton cultivation, while South of it, very little attention is paid to the production of tobacco, while the western part of the State from the richness of its grasses, and the luxuriance of its vines rivals, and from the superiority and the greater mildness of its climate, more than rivals the best pastures of the North. I may add here, that quarries of exceedingly beautiful marble are said to be found in Cherokee county the most westerly county of North Carolina.

But now for your horticulture. First, let me observe this town is called the city of oaks from the number of these trees, original tenants of the soil, which the first settlers of the town and the present residents that have succeeded them, had the good taste to preserve. To me there are few objects of greater grand beauty than one of these aborigines of the forest, with his "fifty arms so strong," clothed in their full fresh vendure of May or early June, relieved against the deep, deep blue, and serene sky of this climate.

There is in addition the artificial beauty arising from cultivation. Except in the mere business part of the place, there are few houses without their front lot for ornamental and their back lot for kitchen gardening. Very many houses have attached to them, conservatories filled with exotics. Even where these are not found, the front yards are kept by careful attention in rich grasses, sometimes green (as the Kentucky grass for instance) through the whole winter, with trees of various descriptions, deciduous and evergreen, with borders of shrubbery and ornamental flowers.

But come, let us hasten, after this long delay, to what you will be more interested in, the practice of the kitchen garden. Let us enter my garden. You see, that being originally a sloping lot of ground, it was necessarily terraced. Let us sit at the corner of this bank, faced with the Kentucky grass. Look around! You perceive there has been an attempt to unite the dulce with the utile, the ornamental with the necessary; the decoration of the parlor with the preparation of the kitchen—the former, principally with the care of the fairer sex of my household, the latter I have taken under my own charge. This bed on the left is one of hyacinths, now out of bloom. On each side of the main walk we have passed through, are rows of choice roses of several varieties, and of almost every hue. Many of them, as you see, will soon be in bloom. Interspersed among the roses, are flowering shrubs; vines and roots of many kinds. Off to the right, are climbing roses, with a Chinese honey-suckle, and what is popularly called, "the yellow jessamine," but which is really, as a very learned friend of mine, an eminent botanist, Dr. Curtis, of Hillsboro, writes in his admirable practical work, "the Woody plants of North Carolina," a "*Gelsemuona sempervirens*". Read what he says of it:

"Its graceful evergreen leaves, the profusion of its large, bright and deliciously fragrant blossoms, renders this vine the pride of our forest."

Immediately behind us is a bed of potatoes, the common potatoes of course, not the sweet. A great part of them are up, but I am afraid a late frost has very much injured them. I planted them in December of last year, according to my usual and generally successful practice. Hereafter, I shall not plant till the peach tree is in bloom, generally the beginning of March.

Beyond those two beds of Asparagus immediately before you, is a plot of Wakefield cabbages, sown the first week of last November. In the severity of the winter, they were covered with glass. Have I Winningstadts? Certainly. I consider them the finest early though not the earliest Spring cabbage. My Winningstadts are on the last plot in the garden to the right. I sow in November, as being the earliest time to prevent many of my plants running to seed. Yes, I have also a few early cauliflowers. If they succeed they will bloom in May. Between the rows of cabbage, you see is lettuce, the early cabbage lettuce, sowed in September, at the same time with spinach and black mustard, and onion seed. Do the young onion plants endure the winter? Perfectly, as you will presently see. So does the spinach; so does the mustard, without any covering; and the lettuce. I cultivate two other kinds of lettuce, besides that you see so large, the Ice lettuce, called so, I suppose, from the semi-transparency of its ribs. A delicate lettuce of fine flavor, but of short continuance, as it endures neither heat nor cold well, and soon runs to seed. The other is the large India, taking all its qualities into consideration, the best lettuce I have ever met with. It does not endure cold remarkably, but it does heat. The cabbage lettuce we have been eating for more than a month. You see it is now well headed. We have had asparagus for some days, and are now on our second crop of radishes.

Let us walk around some of the plots. I indulge a great deal, you see, in pears, some dwarf and some standards. The pear is a delicious fruit and is almost the only tree-fruit not infested by insects. The peach in the garden is destroyed by the curculio, and the apple both by the curculio and the cod-line moth.

This mammoth bush as you term it, but which is no bush but a tree in the eastern and southeastern part of the State where the climate is somewhat milder, is the fig, and a most valuable fellow. He is never infested by insects, always bearing a delicious fruit. When the frost does not interfere, bearing a first and always a later second crop. In this altitude so far up the country, the plant is sometimes injured by the frost, but never entirely destroyed.

The strawberries are of various sorts, most of them are in full bloom, so are my early peas. I shall have them both, early in May.

The grapes are Catawba and Isabella. The Isabellas scarcely ever ripen well. The Catawbas sometimes succeed remarkably well. As you perceive this year I mulch them with oak leaves; as I think it is what is principally needed to prevent rot. One year I suffered weeds to grow among my grapes, and merely cut them down without attempting to weed them up. I had that year a great quantity of grapes; last year I took particular pains to keep the ground clean and I had few or no grapes. But "part hoe" is not necessarily "proper hoe." I shall try however, the leaves. I will shew you soon a native, on which like the true native man of the State you can rely. In the meantime here are my tomatoe plants set out from a cold-frame; I never used a hot-bed, as in this climate it is I think unnecessary and dangerous, unless you have a gardner you can certainly trust. Here are my cucumbers, removed from the frame on inverted sods, as are also melons and squashes. You see my spinach is going to seed and so is my autumn sown mustard. And here is the grape vine, the Scuppernong. Not of the highest character for either the press, or the table. I doubt its being ever made a good wine grape, not of exquisite flavor, as the Hamburg, not of high Patrician standing, but of good steady, regular, useful, sober, yeomanly qualities. Its bloom is after all frosts are over, no insects infest it; it spreads and bears to any extent you please to carry it and regularly. But I must warn you, that it is a downright Southerner and steadily refuses to bear at all beyond Mason's and Dixon's line. Nay, I am not sure that he will condescend to bear in Virginia. I believe he looks with a good deal of indifference upon the pretensions of the

F. F's. In fact he is a genuine native North Carolinian and is truer to his native State than many a North Carolina man or woman.

The poles before you are for Lima beans, recently planted but not yet up.

And now I have told you nearly, if not quite all, you wished to know. I will only add if you go south or east from Raleigh, the products of the garden are earlier; if north or west later than they are here. "*Auream quisquis mediocritatem diligit Tutus.*" Take the gold mean of Raleigh with its undoubted salubrity, and come and live among us.

R. S. MASON.

FACTS FOR EMIGRANTS and CAPITALISTS.

THE SWAMP LANDS OF NORTH CAROLINA.

1,500,000 ACRES,

In the Eastern portion of North Carolina lying on the Atlantic Ocean, from Virginia to South Carolina, there are millions of acres of Swamp lands in their native forest growth, of great fertility and value. Most of these lands can be bought from their present proprietors at nominal prices, not one-third their real value.

The Board of Literature of North Carolina holds in trust for the benefit of Public Education all those swamp lands which belong to the State, supposed to contain one million five hundred thousand acres. These lands are for sale. Besides these, there are many millions of acres owned by private persons and corporations, which can be purchased. For specific information in reference to these lands, apply to the North Carolina Land Company, *Raleigh, N. C.*

In 1867, the Board of Literature of North Carolina, prepared and published a description of the State Swamp lands from official sources. As this description holds good in most particulars in reference to all the swamp lands of Eastern North Carolina, we deem it proper to present to our readers the following statements from that document published by the Board of Literature:

GENERAL DESCRIPTION.

The term *Swamp* is applied in North Carolina to low, wet and spongy lands unfit for cultivation without thorough drainage. The statute meaning of the term is a large body of such land; and it is applied to districts in the alluvial region of the State not affected by tide or salt water that can be drained.

Some of the lakes are isolated, and others are found within the swamps and occupying their highest points; and all of these lands are susceptible of thorough drainage, the expense *per* acre being much less where large bodies are drained by one system of canals. This is one main reason why many of these lands have not hitherto been improved: for the swamps are too large for single proprietors, and the cost *per* acre of draining a single plantation, of moderate size, would generally be more than three times that of draining an entire district.

The lands are all level, and, being alluvial, are free of stones and pebbles, and, when improved, of very easy tillage.

SPECIFIC QUALITIES.

The swamp lands described above may be divided, with reference to soil, production and value, into three general classes.

FIRST.—The *very fertile*, of which the improved lands of Hyde county are the general type, and for a scientific description of which, of the highest authority, the reader is referred to the following:

SWAMP LANDS OF THE HYDE COUNTY TYPE: SCIENTIFIC AUTHORITY.

The late E. Emmons, LL D., formerly of the Geological Survey of New York, and well and favorably known to the scientific world, was, at the time of his death, and for years before had been, State Geologist of North Carolina.

He examined with much care the agricultural characteristics of the swamp region of North Carolina, subjecting the soils to a thorough analysis, and personally inspecting their cultivation and production.

From an elaborate report made in 1858, the following extracts are taken:

"Maize (Indian Corn) must be ranked among the most exhausting crops; and it is evident that poor soils will scarcely repay the farmer for its cultivation. * * *
While it must be admitted that maize is an exhausting crop, it is equally clear and conclusive that it is one of the most important and valuable, and hence it may be regarded as one which pays the best. * * * * *

The foregoing remarks respecting the maize crop have been

made in consequence of the peculiar adaptation of the soil of Hyde County to this cereal. It is the granary of the South. It is true that the number of bushels *per* acre which constitute the average crop is less than the number frequently made on other kinds of soil. Thus, a hundred bushels of corn may be grown upon an acre, but the Hyde County soils rarely exceed sixty bushels *per* acre; but from fifty to sixty bushels are grown, annually, *per* acre for an indefinite term of years, without the expense of fertilizers, while the heavy premium crops require a great expenditure on them; and these have to be repeated, in order to keep the ground in a good condition; and hence, in the long term of years, the profits of these rich lands greatly exceed those which are only moderately so, naturally, and require, every few years, an instalment of manure."—*Report of* 1858, *pages* 28*th*, 29*th*.

"The Hyde County soils have acquired a deservedly high reputation.

Some tracts have been cultivated over a century, and the crops appear to be equally as good as they were at an early period of their culture; and yet no manure has been employed, and they have been under culture in Indian corn every year, or what would be equivalent thereto. * * *

In accomplishing the object of my visit, I was ably seconded by Dr. Long, of Lake Landing, who has become the owner of a tract which has borne this crop, (Indian corn,) for one hundred years without manures. It does not seem to have deteriorated by this long cultivation; or the crops do not *show* a peceptible falling off; still, there has been a large consumption of materials during the one hundred years of cultivation, which may be made to appear by analysis.

The great supply of nutriment, however, still holds out, and the one hundred years to come, if subjected to no greater drains upon its magazine of food, will, at such a distant period, continue to produce its ten to twelve barrels of corn to the acre."—*Ibid*, *pages* 19—21.

"In Onslow, the White Oak Desert is the most interesting tract of swamp land in the County, and is at the head of White Oak Creek. This tract may be drained into Trent River. The timber is very large, and consists of white oak, poplar and pine.

The most important work which has been undertaken, is the drainage of a part of this tract by Mr. Franck. He has been able to secure two objects, the drainage of the land, and a good water power, with a fall of about twelve feet.

The thickness of the soil in Mr. Franck's poccosin (swamp)

is five feet towards the outer rim, and still thicker towards the middle, attaining at least ten feet of rich soil. * *

The excellent quality of parts of it, which are covered with heavy timber, proves by cultivation that it is equal to the Mattamuskeet lands of Hyde—their average yield being twelve barrels of corn to the acre."—*Ibid, pages* 37—38.

This White Oak Desert, or Swamp, lies partly in Onslow and partly in Jones County, consists of about ninety-four thousand acres, and belongs to the Literary Board.

* * "The fertility of the lands drained by Mr. Franck, although on the edge of the swamp, and not so rich as in the interior, fully sustains the analysis of Professor Emmons, and the deductions therefrom, that they 'were equal in value to the best quality of the Hyde County soils.' They have yielded, as I am informed by Mr. Franck, every year, an average of from ten to twelve barrels of corn per acre, or twelve hundred pounds of seed cotton; and last year an elderly negro man, who cultivated a portion on shares, with two young negro women and a boy, all of whom, including the man himself, were stricken down with the small pox, made six bales of cotton and two hundred and forty barrels of corn."—*Gen. Gwynn's Report to the Literary Board in* 1867.

"The swamp lands of Brunswick and New Hanover, and adjoining Counties, resemble, in many respects, those of Hyde and Onslow. The earthy matter is as fine as that of Onslow or Hyde County lands, and its quality and condition prove the same capacity, as it appears to me, for a productive cultivation for a series of years."—*Dr. Emmons.*

Gen. Walter Gwynn, one of the most eminent and experienced civil engineers of the United States, and who, for many years, has been engaged in the various departments of his calling, in different States of the Union, has been several times in the employment of the Literary Board of North Carolina. He has surveyed a number of its Swamps, and in a report made to the Board, in 1867, says:

"I am unable to state with precision what proportion of the State lands, amounting in all to about a million and a half of acres, belongs to the class that comes up to the standard of the Hyde County or Mattamuskeet lands. I feel confident, however, that it exceeds somewhat a fourth, and that a large proportion of the remainder, though falling below this standard, is equal to the average quality of lands in the country, known and regarded as good lands.

The rest would be valuable as manures for other lands, and

for peat, which has lately become an article of commerce from the neighboring swamps of Virginia."

"It will be useful to compare the swamp lands (of North Carolina) with the prairies of Illinois, whose characteristics have drawn westward so many emigrants from New England, New York and the old world. The swamp soils of North Carolina show a greater capacity for endurance than the prairie soils of Illinois, notwithstanding the annual crop is somewhat less *per* acre; but on the score of location we are unable to see that the Illinois soils have a preference.

As it regards health, Hyde County is no more subject to chills and fevers than the country of the prairies. It is a remarkable fact that persons live and labor in swamps with impunity, or freedom from disease."—*Dr. Emmons.*

All things considered, these lands are among the most desirable in the world: they produce grass and fruits as well as cereals, are of easy cultivation, and are tilled from generation to generation, without showing any signs of exhaustion.

They are generally covered with a heavy and dense growth of timber, vines, reeds and grass; the soil is from five to fifteen feet deep, and consists of decomposed vegetable matter, fine sand, and finely comminuted clay. It produces exuberantly all the grains, grass, cotton, rice, pease, potatoes, turnips, pumpkins, melons, the garden vegetables, apples, peaches and grapes; but the test of its fertility is its growth of Indian corn, an exhausting crop, which it will yield in large amounts, from year to year, without manures or stimulants, and for an indefinite period.

It will not produce as much *per* acre as the heavy clay soils in the highest state of improvement; but considering the difference in the expense of production, the crops of the former are vastly the more profitable.

The average yield of Indian corn *per* acre, without the application of fertilizers or stimulants, is from fifty to seventy-five bushels; and experience has proved that this will continue, from year to year, for more than a century, while science infers, from the facts of the past and from careful analyses, that even two centuries of close cultivation will not exhaust the natural and ever renewing fertility of these soils.

SECOND.—Intermediate soils, partaking somewhat of the nature of the first class, and something, also, of that of the third.

Swamps of this character sometimes contain highly fertile fringes, or districts, alternated with sections of sandy lands not productive, or with peaty soils, devoid of timber; but generally the lands included under this head are of medium quality, producing the same growth with those of the first, but in less abundance.

They would be regarded as very valuable but for their proximity to the best soils of the world; and many of them are more peculiarly adapted to wheat and the finer grasses than the lands of the first class; and their average yield of Indian corn, which is about twenty-five to forty bushels *per* acre, can be cheaply and easily increased by the application of fertilizers which abound in this region.

They are, like the lands of the first class, of very easy tillage; and one good application of the marl, which is found in this section in exhaustless quanties, will add to their productiveness for twenty years.

For further particulars, and a more scientific description, read again the foregoing description of the First Class.

THIRD.—This class embraces what is usually known in North Carolin, as Open Ground Swamp, being destitute of woody growth, not inundated with water, but always saturated with moisture.

The soil consists of organic or undecomposed vegetable matter, and not productive in its present state; but when turned up to the sun, acted on by caustic lime, and packed by cultivation, it becomes in many instances very fertile.

But it is due to say that the process necessary to the productiveness of these lands are not likely to be applied at present in a region abounding in soils that need no improvement except a thorough drainage; and they are now valuable chiefly as vast repositories of peat, easily and cheaply obtained, and near to water carriage, and as exhaustless beds of manures for other soils deficient in the elements of which they consist.

These prarie lands are described more fully as follows:

" Some of the swamps are open, or marsh lands; the surface is usually destitute of timber, and covered with a coating of moss, or a growth of reeds and briars. These open lands were once, without doubt, clothed with a large and heavy growth of trees, which have, in the course of time, been prostrated by fire. * * * * The moss has a highly refractive quality, and almost entirely excludes the soil below from the influence of the sun: evaporation goes on slowly, the ground is kept full of water, vegetation checked, and what few seeds remain are so chilled as to destroy germination. * * * * The soil thrown up on the banks of drains, made into the open lands, produces a growth of bushes and weeds of the greatest vigor and luxuriance, and the only things requisite to render the

the open lands fertile are drainage and cultivation. The moss which now covers their surface, instead of being injurious, will, with lime dressing, make a coating of manure of immense value."—*Report of Hon. A. Nash, Engineer in* 1827 *to the Board of Internal Improvement of N. C.*

"Peat is one the most common materials which has been employed as a fertilizer, and has received the same sanction of those who have used it."—*Dr. Emmons' Report of* 1860, *page* 59.

The Board of Literature owns a swamp of this kind con taining 87,000 acres, lying on navigable water, and within a few miles of Beaufort, one of the best harbors on the Atlantic coast. The peat here is of the finest quality, and rich in the elements of fertility needed by more sandy lands.

INCIDENTAL ADVANTAGES OF THE SWAMP LANDS OF NORTH CAROLINA.

I. THEIR NATURAL GROWTH.

Some of the swamps contain large bodies of timber, such as pine, juniper, cypress, oak, poplar, ash and gum; and in a region accessible to market, such products of the forest are of great value. The business of timber getting has ever been profitable in Eastern North Carolina; the best markets for lumber are comparatively near, and the trees are of the most valuable kind, and often as large and fine as any in the world.

Grapes, valuable for wine and for table use, abound; and it is only necessary to specify the Scuppernong, famous over the continent, and which grows wild in immense quantities, and on vines that grow to immense size, and attain to a great age.

The reeds and grass of the swamps afford a rich natural pasturage for cattle during the whole year, and this species of stock can be raised as cheaply and abundantly as in any other ction of the country.

II. MARL BEDS.

The alluvial region of North Carolina abounds in immense beds of shell marl, a species of fertilizer exactly suited to the soils of this section.

The marl is found near the surface, and often begins with it, reaching generally to a considerable depth, and the beds contain hundreds and sometimes thousands of tons which can be easily and cheaply removed.

One good dressing of this fertilizer will materially add to

the productiveness of the land for twenty years; and thus nature has deposited within this favored region the means of increasing and perpetuating the fertility of the soil.

III. THE FISHERIES.

Fish, oysters, turtle, and a valuable species of terrapin, abound in eastern North Carolina; and here are found the largest fisheries of shad, herring and rock, on the American continent. Mullets, and other desirable varieties of fish, are, also, caught in great quanties; and the numerous sounds, lakes, rivers and creeks teem with an inexhaustible supply of food for the sustenance of human life.

It is, also, worthy of note that wild fowl and game of other kinds exist in such quantities as to form an article of trade with other States; and as an illustration of the extent of the fisheries, and of their value, it may be mentioned that during the present year one hundred and seventy-five thousand herrings have been taken at a single haul of the seine.

IV. ADVANTAGES FOR RAISING BEEF AND PORK.

It has already been stated that cattle can be raised as cheaply and as numerously here as in any part of the country; and it should be added that the facilities for producing pork are equally great. Indian corn, the staple food for fattening hogs in the west, can be grown here on as extensive a scale and at little expense as in any part of the world: and in addition to this, eastern North Carolina produces another article nearly as valuable for stock as corn, and which cannot be raised to advantage in the cold States of the west.

One of the most nutritious, healthy and delightful of all vegetables used for the food of man and beast is the sweet potatoe; and in the region under discussion it requires little care or culture, and on soils comparatively poor, from two to five hundred bushels *per* acre can be easily raised.

V. FACILITIES FOR RAISING FRUITS AND GARDEN VEGETABLES FOR THE MARKETS OF NORTHERN CITES.

The peach tree is not so healthy in the alluvial region as on the stiff clay soils in the hill country; but the fruit matures so much earlier than in the Northern States, that it can be raised to great profit for the city markets.

There is an apple peculiar to the Hyde region which is of superior quality and one of the best keepers in the world: it is called the Matamuskeet, grows luxuriantly in the section referred to, and of which it is a native, and may be kept all the year round without rotting.

But along the numerous navigable waters of this region there is the best opening in the world for profitable gardening; vegetables of all kinds can be produced in vast quantities, and of the best quality, and placed in the markets of Boston, New York, Philadelphia, &c., &c., and weeks before they will mature on the vastly more expensive lands in the vicinity of those cities.

VI. EASE WITH WHICH THE SOIL MAY BE CULTIVATED.

It is no small item in the comparative advantages of this region, that the soil, when once prepared for cultivation is as mellow and friable as a bed of ashes. One man and a small horse or mule can till as much ground, as a hand and a half, or a man and boy, and two heavy draught animals, will do in the west; and less expense is necessary for agricultural implements of every kind than in stiff clay or rocky soils.

VII. FACILITIES FOR GETTING TO MARKET.

This favored region combines advantages seldom found together, perhaps not combined, on such a scale, in any other place.

The forests furnish resources for foreign trade equal to that of the regions where timber is the chief article of export; the fisheries add another great staple to commerce, and beef and pork furnish others.

Cotton may be grown as profitably as in the valley of the Mississippi, and corn as abundantly as in the richest States of the west.

To these may be added grapes and other fruits, wine, and garden vegetables; *and all these things are produced in comparative proximity to the markets where they command the best prices.*

Nearly all eastern North Carolina is convenient to navigable water, and the whole of it is near to the Atlantic ocean; and the great staples of this region yield a much better price to the producer than in any other section where they are so largely produced. When, for instance, corn is worth to the producer in Illinois or Iowa but fifteen cents *per* bushel, it yields sixty to seventy-five to the farmer in eastern North Carolina; and so with other products

For the same reason the inhabitants of this region obtain their foreign supplies at much cheaper rates than they can be furnished to the people of the west; and to all this it must be added that building materials and fuel are vastly less expensive, the working season longer, and all seasons milder.

VIII. CLIMATE AND HEALTH OF THE COUNTRY.

The latitude of all parts of North Carolina is that most favorable to out-of-door labor and exposure, and to the prolongation of human life.

The statistics of the Census of the United States prove that the average duration of human life is as long in North Carolina as in any part of the world; and the eastern part of the State is not an exception to this general salubrity.

This assertion is based on facts and on the investigations of science; and it is freely made in view of the most ample opportunity on the part of the world of verifying its accuracy.

The swamps of eastern North Carolina do not generate the malaria which, in the marshy regions further south, causes malignant fevers; and the experience of a large population devoted for over a century to open air pursuits, will confirm the statement that the laborers here, in the woods, in the fields and on the waters, are generally as healthy as in any part of the country.

The subject needs no ingenious bolstering; conclusive facts are within the reach of all and will speak for themselves.

The winters are not so rigorous as in higher and drier localities in the same latitude, the climate being tempered by the influences of the Gulf stream, and the proximity of the ocean; and the same causes, also, reduce the heats of summer, and aid in promoting the healthfulness of the climate.

The region will be found to be suited to laborers from Germany and the British Isles; and natives of the South of Europe will find health, and congenial and profitable employment, in this favored region.

The following facts sustain this assertion:

HEALTH OF LABORERS IN THE SWAMP REGION OF N. CAROLINA.

"It may be inferred that, as the swamp lands are so low and wet, they must necessarily be extremely unhealthy, or become so when drained, and the vegetable matter begins to decompose. Experience, however, does not support this view. The testimony of those who have cultivated them for forty years is, that their families have enjoyed as much health as their neighbors who have lived at a distance. Persons who are in the habit of plunging into the swamp lands knee deep for draining, and when drained, to live in the immediate vicinity of the black vegetable mould for years, are rarely sick with fevers. * * * Miasms, which generate fever, arise more from the banks of rivers than from the swamp and poccosin soils."—*Report of Dr. Emmons, in* 1858, *page* 57.

A fact mentioned by the late Gen. W. A. Blount is of great importance; it is, that for forty years during which he had been a resident upon this class of lands, the health of his family, white and black, will compare favorably with those in the healthiest localities in eastern North Carolina.

The late Edmund Ruffin, of Va., eminent for his practical contributions to agricultural knowledge, says:

" From the existing conditions of the land and water of this lake region, every stranger would infer the general and worst effects of malaria in producing disease and death. But I was assured that such was not the fact, and that the residents suffered but little from autumnal diseases.

And this I could readily believe, even after making proper allowances for the too favorable view as to health, which every man takes of his own place of residence. The people I saw had the appearance of enjoying at least ordinary good health. Among the number that I saw there were three neighboring resident proprietors, each of seventy or more years of age, and then in good health. Few of the residents move to, or visit, the high lands in the autumn, and these few for short times, and more in pursuit of pleasure than of health."

To these evidences may be added the authoritative testimony of Gen. Walter Gwynn.

In an official report to the Literary Board, he says:

" These facts corroborate the views advanced by Dr. Charles E. Johnson, in an admirable address on malaria, delivered before the Medical Society in 1851, and are conformable to my own experience. As chief Engineer of the State, I was engaged in draining swamp lands in Tyrrell County, from 1839 to 1843, a period of three years. The main features of this drainage consisted in lowering lakes Pungo and Alligator, each five feet. This was effected by cutting canals twenty-five and thirty feet wide respectively, which drained a surface of about 70,000 acres that was covered with water. Lateral canals were then cut twelve and sixteen feet wide, a mile apart. The work was done by contract, the average number of hands employed being about two hundred and fifty, all negroes, with the exception of the overseers and contractors. The latter were constantly exposed to the weather, the negroes worked every day in water and muck, generally knee deep—they, as also, the overseers, were housed in shanties on the banks of the canals—and there was not a single case of fever on the work, nor was the attendance of a physician required in any instance.

In building the railroads from Petersburg to Blakely, from Portsmouth to Weldon, from Weldon to Wilmington, from Wilmington to Manchester, and from Goldsborough to Raleigh, every variety of sandy soils, wet and dry, and every species of marsh, swamp and poccosin soils were encountered and upturned, yet there were but few cases of fever, and they occurred chiefly at Blakely, which was the first terminus of the Petersburg railroad, on the Roanoke river, three miles below Weldon, and on the Great Pee Dee River in South Carolina. The intermediate points were almost entirely exempt, and remarkably so in the valley of the Cape Fear river, opposite Wilmington, where the Manchester road crosses Eagle's Island, through cypress swamps and neglected rice fields. The men employed were chiefly foreigners, disregarded the precautions given them to keep within doors at night, and often slept out on the ground; yet there was not a single case of ague and fever among them, nor did any one of them lose more than two or three days during the entire period they were engaged in the work, which was in the summer and autumn of 1853, and 1854."—*Gen. Gwynn's Report to the Literary Board in* 1867.

IX. STATE OF SOCIETY.

The object in offering for sale the swamp lands of North Carolina is itself a favorable indication of the state of society.

The proceeds of the sales are to be used in re-establishing the prosperous system of Public Schools, temporarily suspended by the results of the late civil war; a system which, up to 1861, had been in existence for twenty years, and by which all the children of the citizens of the State were obtaining an elementary education.

For nine years before the war and during the war it was presided over by a State Superintendent; and it had acquired such a vigorous existence that it lived with all its machinery perfect, through the four years of exhausting strife, and was suspended in 1865, on account of the loss of a large part of its vested funds.

It still has considerable resources, independent of taxation, and which the arts of peace will make available; the people of the State are attached to the principle of universal education, and it is the general purpose to revive the Public Schools and extend their benefits to the children of every race.

The State has made greater progress in education of all kinds, in the last twenty years, than any of her sisters; and the reputation of her schools, and the wholesome state of society, brought pupils to her Academies and Seminaries from the whole southern and south western country.

North Carolina, from her first settlement, has been celebrated for the orderly and reliable character of her inhabitants; she is known, all over the country, as "the good old North," and her people are considered in all America to be pre-eminent for simplicity of manners, consistency of character, and devotion to principle.

They are slow to move, and firm in purpose; and it is known that during the late trying contest of arms, the soldiers of this State were among the most steady, brave and moral to be found on either side.

The State was never factious in politics, and the people never fond of novelties in morals or manners; but the population, as a whole, has been distinguished for obedience to law, fidelity to engagements, and devotion to peace and order.

These are facts known to history, and familiar to all readers of the current literature of the United States; and a society so honorably distinguished in the past still maintains its ancient character, notwithstanding the fiery ordeal through which the whole American nation has been passing for the last few years.

Order reigns supreme, and life and property are as safe here as in any part of the continent; the people are quietly and earnestly devoting themselves to the arts of peace, and a worthy immigrant who comes here from any part of the globe, to join in these avocations, will receive a cordial welcome, and soon find himself at home, and among his friends.

INTRINSIC VALUE OF THE SWAMP LANDS OF NORTH CAROLINA.

"The public archives, running through a period exceeding half a century, exhibit, in regard to the swamp lands, repeated evidences of a high appreciation of their value; and their reclamation has at times engaged the attention of some of the most eminent citizens of the State, and of the country.

Indeed, the utility and vast importance of the undertaking has undergone such thorough and searching investigations, that it would be difficult to present any views that would not be familiar to every intelligent and reflecting man for whom the subject possesses any interest. The late lamented Hon. Edmund Ruffin, of Virginia, in his sketches of Lower North Carolina, presented to the State, and published by order of the Legislature, remarks in reference to the region embracing the lands of the Literary Board: 'All my observations of this great and remarkable agricultural region have brought me to believe that I have not known or heard of any other comparable to it in value.' And after making every allowance for the uncertainty of his grounds, he asserts it as his confident belief, that a system of drainage and improvement suggested, would add hundreds of millions of dollars even to the already great value and wealth of this region."—*Gen. Gwynn's Report to the Literary Board in* 1867.

DRAINAGE OF THE SWAMP LANDS OF NORTH CAROLINA : EASE WITH WHICH IT CAN BE EFFECTED.

"The swamps proper, as heretofore stated, have basin shaped beds, scooped out of the water-glutted sand stratum, which underlies nearly all the land of the tide water region. Those basins, being embedded in a material so surcharged as to be impermeable to water, served at first as the matrix or hot-beds for the formation of the vegetable soils of the swamps. They now serve as receptacles for the down falling rain water, by which they are surcharged and kept so exclusively wet as to be unfit for tillage.

These facts indicate at once the principle of drainage. It consists simply in cutting through the rims of these swamp basins, and extending ditches into the interior deep enough to draw off the water which is in excess some feet below and up to the surface, and by thus removing the before constant saturation, permit the excess of falling rain to sink into the lower earth, and thence pass off below, instead of being kept on or near the surface.

The striking feature of this plan of drainage, worthy of note, is, that owing to the perviousness of the soil, no tap ditches are required to drain off the excess of rain water *over the surface*, the whole of the surplus sinking through and being carried off from below.

Much land is cultivated in corn and produces well, of which the level surface is not more than two and a half feet higher than the water flowing or standing in the ditches.

Mr. Ruffin remarks that 'the ditches dug in this peculiar soil keep open for a long time, and need less labor for repairs and cleaning out than any seen elsewhere. The digging is easy, the open texture of the soil and its great depth make it drain well and far, by lateral percolation, to wherever a lower neighboring outlet is afforded.'"—*Report of Gen. Gwynn in* 1867. *Reports of Engineers Nash, Shaw, Brazier and others confirm these views.*

ADVANTAGES OF THE SWAMP LANDS FOR GRAZING, &C.

"The natural pastures are perennial. The open swamps bear reeds in great quantity and which afford abundant and excellent food for cattle through winter and summer.

For cattle grazing and sheep husbandry Texas only exceeds

it in extent of range; but for raising hogs and fattening them almost without feeding, this portion of the State is greatly and justly valued."—*Gen. Gwynn's Report of* 1867.

"In one respect this region differs from others further from the sea. There is no difficulty in the cultivation of the grasses. It is evident the climate is more humid, and the sea breezes moderate the heat sufficiently in summer to favor the development of this family of plants.

There is no doubt, also, that if the attention of planters was turned to the cultivation of grasses, greater profits might be realized than from the cultivation of maize. It is less expensive, and as hay bears a high price in all the villages of this part of the State, and as there is always a communication with them by water, there can be no doubt that the profits which would arise from hay-making would considerably exceed those of corn.

The green surface of the shores of the lakes, the yards of the houses, and the small pasturages, sustain this view."—*Dr. Emmons.*

Mr. Edmund Ruffin says: "Oats, and especially hay, would be good crops for this humid climate and soil. * * * There is no better country for grasses east of the mountains. In small lots, I saw dry meadows of orchard grass and clover that would have been deemed good in the best grass districts." The writer adds, "the good (and improved) lands are densely populated by an industrious and thriving people, who entertain no doubt of their occupying the richest land in the world—in which opinion they are not far wrong."

FACILITIES FOR GETTING TO MARKET.

"In addition to the peculiar adaptation for agricultural improvement and profit in the land itself, no known region possesses such great facilities for navigation, and for choice of markets.

The whole country is pervaded by broad and deep estuaries near the sounds; and their head-waters make, with their many branches, a net-work of natural and still water canals, as deep, as smooth and as sluggish as artificial canals, and free from the changes of levels and the obstruction of lock-gates which accompany the benefits of canal navigation.

Such great and numerous natural facilities for navigation, as are found in many rivers of this region, are unequalled; and they are excelled by the aid of art only in the canal navigation of the Dutch Netherlands. Most of the rivers receive their head waters from the swamps: and from meteorological observation it is shown, that the great swamps receive from the atmosphere and clouds alone enough water to supply all they retain and all they discharge in rivers. The heavy rains do not speedily pass off as when falling on other lands, and are retained by the absorbent property of the swamp soils: no more than what they cannot imbibe passes off to the small streams, and that which is retained by the slow process of percolation equalizes the supply of the rivers, and keeps their volume nearly uniform throughout both wet and dry seasons."—*Gen. Gwynn's Report in* 1867.

FISH AND FISHERIES OF EASTERN NORTH CAROLINA.

"The abundance, variety and excellence of the fish in the waters of this region are unsurpassed by the same extent in any part of the Atlantic border.

The herring and shad of Croatan and Albemarle Sounds and Chowan river, are proverbially superior in the Southern markets. * * * * The seines used in the different fisheries vary in length from 2,200 to 2,700 yards, and are eighteen feet deep as fished. They are laid out about a mile and a quarter from the shore. Mr. Ruffin says the seine at Stevenson's Point once brought 220,000 herrings at one haul. Terrapin and turtle, also, abound in great plenty."—*Gen. Gwynn's Report in* 1867.

It is wholly unnecessary to multiply proofs of a resource so universally known and acknowledged.

GAME.

Only one illustration will be given of the abundance of profitable game in eastern North Carolina. It is from the pen of the late Edmund Ruffin, of Virginia, venerable, when he wrote, for years, for scientific knowledge, and for his long and useful devotion to the cause of agricultural improvement.

His statements may seem remarkable to any but those familiar with the region referred to; but this proves only the want of general information in regard to the resources of one of the most interesting countries of the world. He says: "Nor is game less abundant. Its extent is scarcely known by any one out of this region. * * * *

There are ducks of various kinds, of which the canvassback is the most esteemed. There are also wild geese and swans. Altogether, they congregate in numbers exceeding all conception of any person who has not been informed. They are often so numerous as entirely to cover acres of the surface of the water, so that observers from the beach would only see ducks and no water between them. These great collections are termed 'rafts.' The shooting season commences in autumn and continues through the winter. The returns in game, killed and secured, through any certain time, to a skillful, and patient, and enduring gunner, are as sure as the profits of any ordinary labor of agriculture and trade, and far larger profits for the capital and labor employed. The following particular facts I learned from the personal knowledge of a highly respectable gentleman and a proprietor on the sound, (Currituck,) in Princess Ann. The shooting, (as a business,) on his shores is done only by gunners hired by himself, and for his own profit, and who are paid a fixed price for every fowl delivered to him, according to its kind, from the smallest or least prized species of ducks, to the rare and highly valued swan. He has employed thirty gunners through a winter. He provides and charges for all the ammunition they require, which they pay for out of their wages. In this manner, he is obliged to know accurately how much ammunition he gives out; and it may be presumed that the gunners do not waste it unnecessarily at their own expense. In this manner, and for his own gunners and his own premises only, in one winter, he used more than a ton of gunpowder, and shot in proportion, which was more than four tons, and forty-six thousand percussion caps.

From this expenditure along the shore of one large farm only, there may be some faint conception of the immensity of the operations, and the results along the shores extending for full one hundred and fifty miles, and on all of which the same business is regularly pursued.

Note by the Editor.—When the foregoing publication was commenced, the precise character of the matter coming from so many sources and at different times, was not known. Beginning with the idea of a small pamphlet, the valuable information elicited from various contributors, has swelled it to a volume. The proprietors have sought truth and truth only from the best sources. The discrepancies in matters of figure and of fact which appear in the work, may be charged to the different stand-points from which the various contributors viewed the facts before them, and the various sources whence they derived their information. One proof of the general truthfulness and correctness of the work, is shown in the singular unanimity of the various writers, thus situated.

Some inaccuracies may have escaped the notice of the Editor, in the hurry of its publication. In the statistical account given of Surry county, the reader will please supply "Dobson," in the place of "Jefferson," which was inadvertently put down as the county-seat of Surry.

At considerable expense the proprietors have added a map of the State, which will be very acceptable to the reader.

Arrangements will be made, if a second edition is called for, to render the work more accurate and thorough.

www.ingramcontent.com/pod-product-compliance
Lightning Source LLC
LaVergne TN
LVHW021413110826
845150LV00007B/1899

* 9 7 8 1 4 2 5 5 1 0 0 5 3 *